The Definitive Sovereign Handbook: Do No Harm, Cause No Loss, Commit No Fraud

Roger Davies

Published by TWON Publications, 2025.

THE DEFINITIVE SOVEREIGN HANDBOOK: DO NO HARM, CAUSE NO LOSS, COMMIT NO FRAUD

First edition. September 27, 2025.

ISBN: 979-8232551377

Written by Roger Davies.

Table of Contents

This book is dedicated to every man and woman who chooses to live in honour when fear would be easier, to speak truth when silence would be safer, and to stand free when others bow to fraud.

It is offered as guidance, not as legal advice, for those who know that conscience is the highest law.

"Law is simple: do no harm, cause no loss, commit no fraud. Everything else is policy."

Introduction

The Three Maxims of Peace

All men and women are born with the same gift. The gift is not given by a government or a king. It is not handed down by a court or signed on a piece of paper. It is the gift of life, and with it comes natural freedom. Freedom is not complicated. It does not require a library of statutes or a web of regulations. It stands on three simple rules that every culture recognises: do no harm, cause no loss, commit no fraud.

These maxims are the whole law when a man or woman lives in honour. You do not need thousands of pages of legal codes to know them. They are written into conscience. They are simple enough for a child to understand, yet strong enough to guide a nation. Every honest tradition, whether in America, Canada, the United Kingdom, or Australia, admits that peace comes when people live by these rules.

Think of the weight of modern law. In the United States, the Code of Federal Regulations runs to more than 180,000 pages. In Canada, statutes and regulations stretch into endless volumes across the federal and provincial levels. In the United Kingdom, Parliament produces new Acts and statutory instruments every week. In Australia, both Commonwealth and state governments fill shelves with legislation that no single human could ever master. People are told ignorance of the law is no excuse, yet no one alive can know all of it. This is a trap.

The maxims cut through that trap. If you do not harm, do not cause loss, and do not commit fraud, you are already standing in the highest law. This is the foundation of sovereignty. When governments and corporations build endless rules, they are building scaffolding around these three principles, but the principles remain. If the scaffolding contradicts them, it collapses. That is why the maxims are not only moral guidelines, they are lawful pillars that reach higher than any statute.

To be sovereign is to live as a man or woman, not as a legal fiction. The state will always seek to draw you into its web of titles, licences, contracts, and procedures. It does this by assuming your consent or tricking you into offering it. Yet when you hold to the three maxims, you carry your authority with you. You do not have to shout, fight, or rebel with violence. You only have to stand in peace, answer with truth, and refuse fraud.

Sovereignty is not about escaping responsibility. It is the opposite. A sovereign accepts full responsibility for every word and every act. You do not blame an employer, a minister, or a judge. You carry yourself in honour. That is why the three maxims are powerful. They keep you from falling into the traps of rage, greed, or deceit.

In the United States, people speak of natural rights endowed by the Creator, rights that cannot be taken or transferred. In Canada, the Charter of Rights and Freedoms claims to secure liberty, yet always subject to such reasonable limits prescribed by law. In the United Kingdom, Parliament claims supremacy, yet the ancient common law still echoes the maxims as the true measure of justice. In Australia, the Commonwealth Constitution speaks of peace, order, and good government, but the real peace rests in men and women who cause no harm or loss and commit no fraud. Across these lands, the words differ but the truth is the same.

Modern society is drowning in rules. Every activity is taxed, licensed, or restricted. You cannot work without paperwork, drive without registration, trade without permission, or even walk freely without being observed by cameras. Every new rule is justified as protection, yet the result is more dependence, more fear, and less freedom.

When you hold to the maxims, you step outside of this fear. You stop asking whether there is a rule for this and start asking whether you are harming, causing loss, or deceiving. That question is simple, and the answer brings peace. The courts cannot fault you when you stand in honour, even if they dislike your position. Officials cannot lawfully claim against you without proving harm, loss, or fraud.

This is not a theory. It is how law itself is built. Every valid claim in every court of record, whether in New York, Toronto, London, or Sydney, requires proof of harm, loss, or deceit. Strip away the ritual and procedure, and this is what remains. The maxims are the skeleton that holds the body of law upright. Without them, the whole thing collapses into arbitrary rule.

This book is not written as a sword to attack. It is written as a handbook to live by. Too many men and women exhaust themselves fighting every notice, every summons, every tax demand. They lose peace in their pursuit of justice. Sovereignty is not about endless conflict. It is about living honourably so conflict fades.

When you learn to live by the maxims, you gain clarity. You see the traps before you step into them. You learn when to answer, when to ask questions, and when to remain silent. You know how to put obligations back on those who make claims. You stop feeding the system with your fear. That is why this book is called a handbook. It is meant to be used daily, not stored on a shelf.

Each chapter will explore the maxims in practical settings: in family life, in community, in commerce, in dealings with officials. It will not matter whether you are in America, Canada, the United Kingdom, or Australia, because the principles are the same. Only the costumes and titles change.

In the United States, state constitutions and federal law grow from English common law, which itself rests on ancient maxims. Judges still quote these maxims when they want to cut through confusion. In Canada, the legal system is split between common law in most provinces and civil law in Quebec, but even there the principle of no harm, no loss, no fraud governs contracts and obligations. In the United Kingdom, centuries of common law decisions show that harm must be proven, that loss must be measured, that fraud destroys consent. In Australia, statutes claim authority, yet the High Court continues to base judgments on equity, fairness, and the prevention of loss or fraud. Across all these lands, a sovereign man or woman who holds to the maxims is standing in the same place, no matter what the statute books say.

Picture a neighbour dispute. In America, two men quarrel over a fence line. In Canada, two farmers dispute water rights. In the United Kingdom, two householders argue over noise. In Australia, two families contest access to a track. In every case, if they remember the maxims, they will ask whether there has been harm, whether there has been loss, and whether there was fraud. If the answer is no, the matter can end in peace. If the answer is yes, they can make remedy without courts by agreeing to restore what was lost or cease the harm. This is law in action. It is not theory. It is not politics. It is the daily life of honourable men and women.

The three maxims are simple to speak but challenging to live. They are not a shield for dishonourable conduct and they are not a trick to escape responsibility. They require courage, patience, and a commitment to truth that does not waver. A man or woman who holds to them will be tested in every area of life. Officials will test them. Neighbours will test them. Employers and creditors will test them. Yet if they remain true, they will not be moved.

The first challenge comes in daily speech. Words are easy to throw yet hard to recall. A sharp tongue can harm more deeply than a weapon. A false statement, even a small one, is fraud. This is why sovereign living begins with speech. If you keep your word, if you speak what is true and useful, you are already living by the maxims. In every jurisdiction, perjury is treated as a grave offence, because it strikes at the foundation of trust. Courts in America, Canada, the United Kingdom, and Australia all agree that a lie under oath destroys the integrity of the process. Yet outside the court, men and women often lie without thought. Sovereignty calls you to hold the same standard in every conversation.

The next challenge comes with property and possessions. Harm is not always physical. Taking what is not yours, damaging another's goods, or trespassing without cause is harm and loss. In every land, theft and damage are punished because they strike at fairness. But law codes are full of confusion about ownership, titles, and registration. Governments often behave as though all property is theirs to tax, seize, or control. A sovereign man or woman knows that possession and use must be honourable. You do not need permission to use your own goods in peace, but you do have a duty not to interfere with the rightful use of others. The maxim cause no loss keeps balance even when statutes are twisted.

Another challenge is found in commerce. Modern trade is bound up with contracts, licences, and complex financial products. Banks create money from signatures. Corporations hide terms in fine print. Governments demand taxes as though every exchange is their business. Yet if you hold to the maxims, you cut through the confusion. Ask whether loss is being caused, whether fraud is present, whether harm results. In the United States, courts often void contracts if fraud is proven. In Canada, unconscionable terms are unenforceable. In the United Kingdom, misrepresentation makes a contract voidable. In Australia, misleading conduct in trade is unlawful. These are different words for the same truth. Fraud destroys consent, and without consent there is no valid obligation.

Officials will often try to draw you into joinder. They act as though the legal name, the licence, or the account is you. They may demand compliance by citing regulations no one has read. They may pressure you to admit obligations you never agreed to. This is where the maxims are most powerful. If you remain peaceful, if you ask calm questions, if you refuse to be drawn into dishonour, their position weakens. In every land, enforcement officers must show lawful authority. Without proof of harm, loss, or fraud, they are only enforcing policy. Policy is not law.

It is important to remember that standing in sovereignty does not mean withdrawing from society. It does not mean refusing every interaction or contract. Life is built on agreements. You may agree to work for an employer, to trade with a shop, to rent or to lend. The difference is that you enter those agreements knowingly and honourably. You do not let fraud or fear guide you. You know that if either side causes loss or harm, remedy must follow. This is the natural balance.

Living by the maxims brings strength in family life as well. Children learn more from example than from lecture. If they see you keeping your word, speaking truth, and resolving disputes in peace, they will grow with the same habits. In America, Canada, the United Kingdom, and Australia, families often struggle under pressure from debt, schools, and government interference. Teaching children the maxims gives them a compass that works even when the outer world is confusing. They will know that as long as they do not harm, do not cause loss, and do not deceive, they stand in honour. That knowledge will protect them better than any statute.

Another field where the maxims show their strength is in dealing with debt and finance. Banks lend credit created from signatures and then claim repayment with interest. Courts enforce these claims as though they are sacred. Yet the maxims expose the fraud. If a man or woman is not told the full truth of an agreement, if terms are hidden, if consent is manufactured by fear, the obligation is not lawful. Fraud vitiates everything. This principle is admitted even in the highest courts of each jurisdiction. The problem is that men and women rarely stand on it with confidence. By living by the maxims, you gain the strength to ask for proof, to demand full disclosure, and to refuse to be bound by deceit.

The maxims also guide you when facing the state itself. Governments act as though they own the people. They issue taxes, fines, and penalties as if they are unquestionable. Yet every claim must rest on proof. If you have not harmed, if you have not caused loss, if you have not deceived, what lawful claim can they make? They may threaten, but threats are not proof. They may presume, but presumption collapses under challenge. This is why notices and questions are so powerful. They shift the burden back onto the claimant, where it belongs. In America, due process requires notice and opportunity to be heard. In Canada, natural justice demands fairness. In the United Kingdom, the right to be heard is ancient. In Australia, procedural fairness is upheld as a principle of common law. All of these ideas stem from the same truth: no man or woman is bound without consent, and consent is destroyed by fraud.

Sovereign life is not about endless confrontation. If you spend all your time arguing with officials, you are still bound to them. The higher path is to live so honourably that their claims cannot touch you. This is why the maxims are practical, not only philosophical. They give you a way to navigate daily life without falling into traps. When you buy, sell, work, or speak, you check yourself against the maxims. When you face disputes, you seek remedy guided by them. When you teach others, you hand down the same compass.

It must be said clearly that standing in sovereignty will test your patience. Officials may mock you, neighbours may not understand, family may worry. The world is trained to believe that statutes are the highest law, that governments are masters, and that men and women are subjects. When you walk a different path, people may resist. Yet peace is stronger than fear. Honour is stronger than deceit. Truth is stronger than threats. In every age, men and women who held to these principles changed the course of history. You are asked to do the same, not with weapons, but with words and conduct.

As you move through this book, you will find each chapter anchored in daily practice. You will see how the maxims guide speech, commerce, family, and community. You will learn how to handle encounters with officials without falling into dishonour. You will learn to recognise fraud, to avoid causing loss, and to hold to peace. The path is not complicated, but it does require consistency.

Sovereignty is not a theory. It is not a philosophy to debate online. It is a way of life. Men and women in America, Canada, the United Kingdom, and Australia share a common heritage of common law and natural justice. That heritage has been buried under statutes and codes, but it is still alive in the conscience of every honest person. By living by the maxims, you awaken that heritage.

At the end of this introduction, the choice is placed before you. You can continue to live by fear of rules you have never read, obeying orders you do not agree with, and submitting to claims you did not consent to. Or you can take the simple path of honour. You can decide that from this day forward you will do no harm, cause no loss, and commit no fraud. This pledge does not require paperwork. It does not require permission. It only requires your will. Speak it aloud if you are ready: I stand as a living man or woman. I will do no harm. I will cause no loss. I will commit no fraud. I live in peace, and I will hold my word in honour.

With that pledge, you are ready to begin the journey. The following chapters will not give you tricks to escape responsibility. They will give you tools to live in freedom with honour. If you follow them with courage and patience, you will find that peace is not granted by government but lived by your own conduct. The three maxims are enough.

Chapter 1
The Sacred Duty of the Living Being

Every man and woman begins life with dignity. That dignity is not granted by a constitution, a parliament, or a court. It is a fact of being alive. From birth, you are more than a number, more than a name printed in capital letters. You are flesh, breath, and spirit. You are not property of a government. You are not a corporate fiction. You are a living being with natural standing.

Yet most of the world has forgotten this truth. From the moment of registration, the state attempts to shift the focus from the living being to a legal entity. A certificate is issued. A record is created. In the United States, this comes as a birth certificate and later a social security number. In Canada, it is a birth registration followed by a social insurance number. In the United Kingdom, a registry entry is made, and a national insurance number is later provided. In Australia, a similar process begins at birth and continues with the issue of a tax file number. In each case, the pattern is the same: the living child is documented, and a paper identity is constructed.

This paper identity is useful for commerce and administration, but it is not the living child. The state, however, treats the paper identity as if it were the person. This is where the confusion begins. Men and women are taught to answer to the paper name without question. They grow up believing the paper entity is them. As adults, they pay taxes, hold licences, and sign contracts in that name, never pausing to ask whether the living being has given full consent.

Sovereignty begins with recognising the difference. You are not the paper. You are not the registration. You are not the corporate entity that officials address in capital letters. You are the living being who can choose whether to stand in honour or to be dragged into dishonour. Once you see this distinction, everything changes.

The state survives on consent. Officials may claim authority, but authority without consent is force. That is why systems are designed to secure your silent agreement. When you accept benefits, when you sign forms, when you fail to object, the state assumes you have consented. In the United States, consent is presumed through your use of identification and signatures. In Canada, by accepting government benefits you are taken to agree to the terms attached. In the United Kingdom, using state services is treated as submission to the law of Parliament. In Australia, engaging with tax and welfare systems binds you to statutory obligations. None of this is disclosed openly, yet it operates everywhere.

This is why the three maxims matter. They allow you to stand without fear, even when surrounded by these systems. If you do no harm, no loss, and no fraud, you have not consented to dishonour. You remain in truth. You remain in peace. You remain outside the traps that officials try to lay.

Standing as a living being also means accepting responsibility. Sovereignty is not an excuse to avoid duty. You are not free to harm others, to cheat in trade, or to speak falsehoods. Many who call themselves sovereign fall into this trap. They think that by rejecting government, they are free of all obligation. This is not honour. Honour is carrying your own weight. Honour is admitting when you have harmed or caused loss and making remedy. Honour is never deceiving.

In the United States, courts still echo this principle when they speak of equity. Equity requires clean hands. You cannot seek remedy while standing in dishonour. In Canada, courts apply the same principle under the idea of fairness. In the United Kingdom, equity is centuries old, guiding judges to deny relief to those who act deceitfully. In Australia, the High Court insists that fraud or bad faith destroys a claim. These are the same truths in different words. To stand in sovereignty, your hands must be clean.

Consider a simple example. A man borrows his neighbour's tool and fails to return it. No harm has been done to the neighbour's body, yet a loss has been caused. The maxim requires remedy. The tool must be returned or replaced. If the man lies and claims he never borrowed it, fraud has been committed. This small matter contains the whole of law. No statute is needed. No police report is required. The principle is simple. Restore the loss. Cease the fraud. Keep peace.

Governments try to complicate what is simple. They regulate borrowing and lending. They issue licences for trade. They tax transactions. They claim jurisdiction over disputes that could be settled by men and women directly. Yet when you step back, the maxim remains. If you cause loss, restore it. If you commit fraud, correct it. If you harm, stop it. All the paperwork in the world cannot change that truth.

Living as a sovereign also means knowing when to speak and when to remain silent. Silence can be taken as consent, but silence used wisely can also protect you from dishonour. If an official demands something that is not lawful, you do not need to argue or fight. You can calmly ask for proof of obligation. If they cannot show harm, loss, or fraud, their claim fails. This works across borders. In America, due process requires proof. In Canada, natural justice demands it. In the United Kingdom, no lawful claim stands without evidence. In Australia, the courts still require substance, not presumption. Your duty is only to remain in honour while refusing what is unlawful.

This path takes practice. The world trains men and women to obey orders without thought. Schools teach children to follow rules, not to question them. Media tells adults to trust authority. Officials rely on fear to secure compliance. Sovereignty requires unlearning these habits. You must learn to question respectfully, to speak truthfully, and to hold your ground peacefully. You must learn to see the difference between the living being and the paper fiction. You must remember that the maxims are enough.

Across jurisdictions, examples abound of men and women who lived this way. In America, communities have settled disputes privately without courts for centuries, relying on common understanding of fairness. In Canada, indigenous traditions of restorative justice mirror the maxims closely. In the United Kingdom, early common law courts were little more than gatherings of neighbours applying the same principles. In Australia, local agreements between settlers and communities often relied on honour rather than statute. These are reminders that law existed long before governments created their codes. Law is not ink on paper. Law is the living practice of peace and honour.

This chapter is about first principles. Before you learn procedures, before you read statutes, before you craft notices, you must ground yourself in these truths. You are not a paper fiction. You are not property of the state. You are a living man or woman with duties and rights that precede government. You stand strongest when you accept responsibility and hold to the maxims. From this ground, everything else becomes clear.

Sovereignty is not a theory to admire from afar. It is a duty that must be lived each day. To say you are free is not enough. Freedom must be matched with honour. The first principle of a living being is to recognise that every act carries weight. Every choice has consequences. To harm another, to deprive another, or to mislead another is to step out of peace. The three maxims are the guardrails that keep you upright on the path.

Many people misunderstand sovereignty. They think it is about resisting government, refusing taxes, or arguing with police. They picture it as endless confrontation. But this is a mistake. Sovereignty is not a battle against officials. It is a way of life that does not depend on permission. The living man or woman who abides by the maxims needs no external master. They carry their own law in their heart. They are not reckless. They are not careless. They are firm, truthful, and peaceful.

The world around you will try to pull you into dishonour. Contracts filled with hidden terms, officials who presume authority, corporations that treat customers as numbers, all invite you to consent without real knowledge. If you are careless, you sign away your freedom. If you are fearful, you submit to threats. But if you hold to the maxims, you cannot be trapped. Fraud cannot bind you if you refuse to play along. Presumption cannot control you if you calmly ask for proof. Harm cannot touch you if you remain peaceful.

In the United States, the doctrine of informed consent is a cornerstone in medicine and contract law. A patient must be told the risks before agreeing to treatment. A buyer must be told the terms before agreeing to pay. In Canada, contracts require meeting of the minds. Without full understanding, there is no agreement. In the United Kingdom, centuries of cases hold that misrepresentation voids a contract. In Australia, courts insist that consent is meaningless if obtained by deceit. These truths show that sovereignty is not rebellion. It is alignment with the highest principles already admitted in every jurisdiction.

The duty of the living being extends beyond legal matters. It covers daily interactions. When you greet a neighbour, do so in peace. When you sell or buy, do so in fairness. When you work, do so with honesty. In every case, the maxims apply. If you slip and cause harm, admit it and restore peace. If you cause loss, replace it. If you err with words, correct them. Honour grows by practice. It is not the absence of mistakes. It is the willingness to make remedy when mistakes occur.

Sovereignty also demands courage. There will be times when standing in truth feels dangerous. Officials may threaten arrest. Employers may threaten dismissal. Creditors may threaten court. Friends and family may urge you to submit for convenience. Yet honour is not convenience. Honour is the willingness to stand even when it costs you. History is full of men and women who chose peace over submission. In every land, their names endure while the names of their oppressors fade.

One of the hardest lessons for sovereign men and women is patience. The system is designed to frustrate. Letters go unanswered. Questions are ignored. Cases are delayed. Officials use time as a weapon, hoping you will give up. But patience is part of honour. To stand without giving up, to keep your word even when others break theirs, is strength. In America, those who have fought unjust foreclosures often prevail only after years of persistence. In Canada, cases of wrongful dismissal have shown that perseverance exposes the truth. In the United Kingdom, ordinary people have resisted unlawful council demands with patient notices until the claims dissolved. In Australia, men and women have used steady questioning to outlast officials who rely on intimidation. The maxim is not speed. The maxim is honour.

Responsibility also means caring for yourself. Harm includes self-harm. To abuse your body with excess, to destroy your health, or to numb your conscience is dishonourable. A sovereign does not hand control of their mind or body to substances, to propaganda, or to fear. Freedom requires clarity. You cannot stand firm if you are clouded. To live as a sovereign is to guard your health, to strengthen your mind, and to act with intention.

Consider again the difference between the living being and the legal fiction. The legal fiction has no conscience. It cannot live by the maxims. It is a tool used by the state for administration. The living being has conscience. That conscience is the voice of law within. If you confuse yourself with the fiction, you forget conscience. You obey orders and statutes without question. If you remember that you are living, you recall that conscience outranks code. That is the essence of sovereignty.

This understanding is not confined to one nation. Across borders, the pattern repeats. In the United States, people are taught to identify with a social security number. In Canada, with a social insurance number. In the United Kingdom, with a national insurance number. In Australia, with a tax file number. Yet none of these numbers describes the living being. They are tools for administration, not marks of identity. Officials may address you through them, but you are free to answer as the living being, not as the fiction. You may accept contracts when honourable. You may refuse when fraudulent. You may live in peace without being absorbed by the system.

The duty of the living being is also to guard community. Sovereignty is not isolation. It is not selfishness. A man or woman who lives by the maxims strengthens their community by example. Neighbours see that disputes can be settled peacefully. Children see that truth matters more than convenience. Friends learn that honour holds even when it costs. This is how societies change. Not by revolution, but by millions of quiet acts of sovereignty.

The three maxims are not complicated. A child can recite them. Yet they are deep enough to guide a lifetime. Every religion, every culture, every tradition points to them in some form. Do unto others as you would have them do unto you. Speak the truth. Restore what you take. Keep peace. These sayings echo the same law. Governments may bury them under codes, but they cannot erase them. The living being who remembers them carries true law wherever they go.

At the close of this chapter, pause and reflect on your own life. Have you caused harm by words or acts? Make remedy. Have you caused loss by neglect or carelessness? Restore it. Have you deceived, even in small matters? Correct it. This is the first step of sovereignty. Before you stand against the world, stand true within yourself. Honour begins at home. Once you have cleaned your own house, you can stand firm before others.

The sacred duty of the living being is not glamorous. It is not dramatic. It is steady, humble, and constant. To do no harm, to cause no loss, to commit no fraud, day after day, builds strength. With time, officials cannot shake you, neighbours cannot unsettle you, and fear cannot rule you. You are sovereign because you live in honour. That is the true beginning of freedom.

Chapter 2
Speech Without Injury

Words carry power. Long before paper contracts, long before governments issued statutes, men and women bound themselves by their word. To speak falsely was dishonour. To speak with truth was law. Every culture knew this. Every court in history has punished perjury more harshly than simple mistakes, because speech is the channel through which trust flows.

To live by the maxims, you must master your speech. Harm often begins not with blows, but with words. A lie, a threat, a false accusation can harm more deeply than any weapon. In America, slander and libel are actionable in court, for they recognise the injury caused by false words. In Canada, defamation law is similar, and even careless speech that damages reputation can result in remedy. In the United Kingdom, centuries of cases have drawn fine lines between free expression and injurious falsehoods. In Australia, courts balance free political speech with the duty not to destroy another's standing through lies. These examples show that in every jurisdiction, the law recognises the power of speech.

The sovereign man or woman does not wait for a judge to enforce this truth. You live it daily. You do not speak to wound. You do not deceive with words. You do not cause loss through false claims. Instead, you speak with clarity and peace. You keep your word, and if you fail, you make remedy. This is honour.

There is a saying in the United States that a man's word is his bond. In Canada, contracts sealed by handshake once carried the same weight as written documents. In the United Kingdom, the phrase my word is my bond echoed through centuries of trade and commerce. In Australia, oral agreements are still enforceable when backed by witness. These traditions remind us that speech creates obligations. To speak falsely is fraud. To break one's word without remedy is loss. To speak threats that cause fear is harm.

Many sovereign men and women lose strength by careless talk. They argue with officials. They shout in anger. They make wild claims they cannot support. This is not the way of honour. When you speak rashly, you step into dishonour. You give officials weapons against you. You bring confusion into your own camp. Better to speak little, but with weight. Better to ask questions than to make claims. Better to pause than to let anger speak for you.

In America, the right to remain silent is protected under the Fifth Amendment, a shield against self incrimination. In Canada, section 7 of the Charter protects the right to life, liberty, and security, which includes silence when questioned. In the United Kingdom, the right to silence has been weakened by statutes, yet courts still require that confessions be voluntary. In Australia, the privilege against self incrimination remains strong. These rules admit a simple truth: words spoken without care can bind you, trap you, or condemn you.

The sovereign does not treat silence as weakness. Silence can be the strongest form of speech. When asked to contract without proof, silence is refusal. When accused without evidence, silence is strength. Yet silence must not be used to hide dishonour. If you have caused harm or loss, silence is fraud. You must admit and make remedy. The balance is delicate, but the maxims guide you.

Words also create peace. A calm answer can disarm anger. A truthful explanation can dissolve fear. A courteous question can expose fraud without conflict. The man or woman who speaks in peace is often more powerful than the one who shouts. In courts across jurisdictions, those who speak respectfully and clearly are heard more favourably than those who rant. Sovereignty is not bluster. It is the quiet strength of truth spoken without fear.

Speech is also central to contracts. In America, a contract requires offer, acceptance, and consideration. Words alone can create all three. In Canada, the same principles apply, and courts enforce spoken agreements if evidence supports them. In the United Kingdom, oral contracts remain valid when terms are clear. In Australia, the High Court has upheld the enforceability of verbal promises. This shows the responsibility of speech. Every yes and no carries weight. You cannot claim sovereignty while treating words as casual.

Consider a daily example. A neighbour asks for help with a fence, and you promise to assist on Saturday. If you fail to appear without notice, you have caused loss. If you lied when making the promise, you have committed fraud. If your excuse is false, you have harmed trust. Remedy is simple: apologise, explain truthfully, and restore peace. This is how the maxims work in daily life. No statute is required.

Another example is in trade. You sell a used item to a stranger. If you falsely claim it is new, you have committed fraud. If it breaks because you knowingly sold it defective, you have caused loss. If you shout at the buyer when they complain, you cause harm through words. Remedy is to speak truth, admit fault, and restore what was lost. This is simple law, and it is enough.

Speech also binds you to officials. When a police officer asks questions, every word matters. If you argue, you create conflict. If you lie, you commit fraud. If you confess without understanding, you bind yourself. The sovereign response is calm, courteous, and cautious. You ask questions: am I obliged to answer, am I free to go, is there evidence of harm, loss, or fraud. Across America, Canada, the United Kingdom, and Australia, such questions shift the burden back onto officials. They expose the lack of lawful authority without dishonour.

Words can also heal. A man who has harmed another may repair much with sincere apology. In every culture, words of forgiveness restore peace. The maxims are not only shields against dishonour but tools for reconciliation. If you wrong another, you owe them truth. If they wrong you, you offer peace when they repent. This cycle keeps communities strong.

For sovereign living, mastery of speech is not optional. It is essential. Every notice you send, every agreement you enter, every encounter you face depends on words. Whether spoken or written, they are the record of your honour. To speak falsely is to sign a fraudulent contract. To speak truth is to stand as a living man or woman.

To understand the weight of speech, consider how courts across the world treat oaths and affirmations. In the United States, swearing falsely under oath is punished as perjury, with severe penalties. In Canada, the Criminal Code contains similar provisions. In the United Kingdom, perjury has long been treated as one of the most serious crimes against justice. In Australia, lying under oath can carry prison terms. Why is this so? Because the entire structure of courts depends on truthful speech. If words are corrupted, justice collapses. The same truth applies outside the courtroom. Families collapse when words are lies. Communities fall apart when words are used as weapons. Commerce fails when promises are false.

The sovereign man or woman sees speech as sacred. You do not swear lightly. You do not make promises you cannot keep. You do not mislead to gain advantage. These acts may seem small, but they are fraud in seed form. Fraud grows into loss and harm. When you speak falsely, you poison trust. Trust once poisoned is hard to restore.

Governments know the power of words and exploit them. Statutes are written in terms of art, designed to trap the unwary. Words like person, resident, taxpayer, citizen, and driver are defined in ways different from common speech. Men and women answer to them without realising they are stepping into roles created by legislation. In America, the word person is often used in tax codes to include corporations and legal fictions. In Canada, the Income Tax Act defines resident in a way that captures nearly anyone with ties to the country. In the United Kingdom, terms like occupier and liable person in council tax statutes are loaded with hidden meaning. In Australia, drivers are defined under road legislation as those engaged in commercial use, yet the word is applied broadly. These traps show how speech can enslave when used without care.

The way out is awareness. A sovereign asks what a word means before agreeing to it. When an official asks if you are a resident, you ask what they mean by resident. When they call you a person, you inquire what definition they are relying upon. When they accuse you of being liable, you calmly request evidence. This is not argument. It is not defiance. It is speech used with precision to avoid dishonour. By refusing to accept undefined terms, you avoid fraudulent joinder.

Another area where words create bondage is in signatures. To sign is to affirm. Many men and women sign forms, contracts, and statements without reading or understanding them. They trust officials, they fear delay, or they hope to avoid trouble. This is dangerous. Every signature is your word in writing. If you sign falsely, you commit fraud. If you sign without understanding, you risk causing loss to yourself and others. Sovereignty demands that you sign only what is true, clear, and honourable.

In the United States, contract law holds that a signature binds you even if you have not read the terms, unless fraud is proven. In Canada, similar principles apply. In the United Kingdom, courts presume that signing means agreement. In Australia, the High Court has reinforced that ignorance of terms is no defence. These doctrines are designed to bind men and women by their words. The only shield is to refuse to sign what is not true. A sovereign man or woman takes time, reads carefully, asks questions, and alters terms if necessary. Your word is too valuable to waste on false promises.

Speech also shapes your inner world. Words spoken to yourself create belief. If you tell yourself that you are weak, you live as weak. If you tell yourself that you are strong, you grow strong. The maxims apply even here. To speak falsehood to yourself is fraud. To speak defeat into your own life is loss. To speak hatred inwardly is harm. The sovereign disciplines speech both outward and inward. You choose words that align with truth, peace, and honour.

In community, words are the glue. When disputes arise, speech can escalate or heal. A harsh word can ignite a quarrel. A soft word can calm it. In America, community mediation centres rely on dialogue to resolve disputes without courts. In Canada, restorative justice programmes use speech to bring victim and offender together for healing. In the United Kingdom, community resolution schemes favour dialogue over punishment. In Australia, indigenous traditions emphasise circles of discussion to restore balance. All of these rely on honourable speech. Sovereigns live this naturally.

One of the greatest traps of modern systems is fear-based speech. Officials often use threats of fines, prison, or seizure to extract compliance. These words are designed to cause harm by fear. They may have no lawful foundation, but they work when men and women believe them. The sovereign response is to ask for proof. If a tax officer threatens, ask for evidence of obligation. If a police officer threatens, ask for lawful authority. If a judge threatens, ask where harm, loss, or fraud has been proven. Fear dissolves when words are tested.

It is also vital to recognise the difference between opinion and fact. Many people state opinion as though it were truth. This is common in media and politics, where emotion replaces evidence. Sovereigns discipline their speech to distinguish the two. You can share opinion, but you mark it as such. You state fact when you know it to be true. This clarity prevents fraud. In America, defamation law often hinges on whether statements are opinion or false facts. In Canada, fair comment protects opinion, but lies are actionable. In the United Kingdom and Australia, honest opinion defences exist but are narrow. Across all these lands, the principle is the same: false facts harm, but honest opinion spoken as opinion does not.

In daily practice, sovereign speech requires slowing down. Before speaking, ask whether your words will cause harm, loss, or fraud. If the answer is yes, remain silent or change your words. If the answer is no, speak with clarity and peace. This habit transforms your life. People will come to trust you, for they know your word is true. Officials will hesitate to entrap you, for they know you do not speak rashly. Children will imitate you, for they see your consistency.

At times you will fail. You may speak in anger. You may exaggerate. You may promise too much. The test of honour is how you respond. Do you deny and hide, or do you admit and remedy? A sovereign admits, apologises, and restores. This may feel hard, but it builds immense strength. Others learn that your word is not perfection, but it is trustworthy because you repair it when broken.

In closing this chapter, remember that speech is law in motion. Every contract, every oath, every notice, every judgment is speech made solid. If the speech is false, the law is false. If the speech is true, the law is true. By disciplining your words, you discipline your life. By refusing to speak harm, loss, or fraud, you live the maxims. In America, Canada, the United Kingdom, and Australia, courts and communities alike recognise this truth. Sovereignty begins in the tongue. If your words are clean, your path will be clear.

Chapter 3
Encounters With Authority

Every sovereign man or woman will one day face an encounter with authority. It might be a police officer at the roadside, a tax official sending demands, a council employee knocking at the door, or a judge in a courtroom. These encounters are unavoidable. To believe that you can live free of all contact with officials is unrealistic. The question is not whether you will face them but how you will conduct yourself when you do.

The difference between fear and strength in such encounters is preparation. If you approach authority without understanding, fear will rule you. You will be pressured into consent, into contracts you never meant to accept, into admissions you never intended to make. But if you are grounded in the three maxims, you will stand calm. You will know that unless harm, loss, or fraud is proven, no lawful claim exists. You will know that your duty is only to remain in honour, speak truth, and avoid deceit.

In the United States, the Constitution protects against unreasonable searches and seizures, yet millions consent to them because they do not know their rights. In Canada, Charter rights guarantee security of the person, yet men and women surrender it daily by answering questions they were not obliged to answer. In the United Kingdom, police rely on statutes granting wide powers, yet even there, officers must show lawful basis. In Australia, police powers are extensive, but they too collapse without evidence of actual harm, loss, or fraud. Across these nations, the pattern is the same: officials push beyond their lawful authority, and men and women comply out of fear.

The sovereign response is not rebellion but peace. You do not fight officials. You do not insult or threaten them. You stand firm, you remain courteous, and you ask questions. Questions shift the burden back where it belongs. A police officer demands identification. You ask whether you are obliged to provide it, and under what authority. A tax agent threatens penalty. You ask whether they have proof of obligation and evidence of harm. A council worker issues a demand. You ask whether they are making a claim as a man or woman and whether they will accept liability if their claim is false. Each question is polite, but each one removes presumption.

Officials are trained to exploit silence or rash speech. If you say too much, you may confess unknowingly. If you say nothing without explanation, they may treat it as consent. The balance lies in calm questions. You are not refusing. You are not obstructing. You are asking for clarity. In America, this aligns with the right to due process. In Canada, it aligns with the duty of fairness. In the United Kingdom, it echoes the principle that government must prove its case. In Australia, it reflects the requirement that officials act within authority.

Many men and women are intimidated by uniforms, badges, and titles. But these are costumes. Behind every badge is a man or woman who is bound by the same maxims as you. They too must avoid harm, loss, and fraud. If they overstep, they risk dishonour. When you remember this, fear fades. You see that authority is not magic. It is only men and women acting under claim of office. If their claim is lawful, you honour it. If not, you ask for proof.

Consider a roadside stop. In America, police often stop drivers to check licences and registrations. In Canada, roadside checks are common. In the United Kingdom, officers use stop powers under statutes. In Australia, police use road safety laws. In each case, the officer will act as though their request is unquestionable. Many men and women comply without thought. The sovereign does not argue but asks. Am I obliged to answer? Have I caused harm, loss, or fraud? What evidence do you rely on? Such questions shift the dynamic. The officer may still act, but you have preserved honour and record. You have not consented by silence, and you have not dishonoured yourself by anger.

Another common encounter is the tax demand. Revenue agencies in America, Canada, the United Kingdom, and Australia send notices claiming money. Most people pay without question. Yet each demand is only an offer unless supported by proof. A sovereign responds with questions: What obligation are you relying on? Where is the contract? Can you show harm or loss? Such questions are rarely answered directly, but the act of asking preserves your standing. You do not dishonour by ignoring, and you do not consent by paying blindly. You seek truth, and the burden lies with the claimant.

Encounters with authority often escalate because of tone. If you remain peaceful, escalation is harder. If you raise your voice, the official feels justified in using force. Sovereignty is proved in composure. Even in courts, where judges attempt to control proceedings, calm questions can reframe the matter. Asking whether the court is operating under common law, equity, or statute places record on the table. Asking whether harm, loss, or fraud is alleged cuts through layers of procedure.

Officials rely on fear because fear is quicker than law. To resist fear, you must train yourself. Practice calm responses before the encounter comes. Write out questions you can ask in common scenarios. Repeat them until they are natural. Fear weakens when you are prepared.

A man or woman who lives by the maxims does not need to fear authority. Authority is only lawful when it enforces the maxims. When it strays beyond them, it becomes policy, and policy is not law. In America, Canada, the United Kingdom, and Australia alike, courts have struck down unlawful acts of officials. These cases remind us that the maxims still hold, though buried under layers of code.

Encounters with authority test your honour. They are not opportunities to show off knowledge or humiliate officials. They are chances to prove peace. If you remain calm and courteous, you often defuse the situation. Even if the official proceeds against you, you stand without dishonour. You have not lied, you have not consented blindly, and you have not harmed. That is sovereignty in action.

Authority often appears strongest when it is least lawful. A uniform, an office, or a seal gives the impression of power. Yet power without proof of harm, loss, or fraud is only intimidation. The sovereign man or woman learns to see through the appearance and ask for substance. If substance is lacking, you remain in peace.

One of the most difficult encounters is in the courtroom. Many men and women fear courts more than any other place. The setting is designed to intimidate. The judge wears robes. The officials sit higher. The language is formal and unfamiliar. But strip away the costume, and you find the same principle. Every claim must show harm, loss, or fraud. If the court cannot show this, it is theatre.

In America, due process demands that courts establish jurisdiction and evidence. In Canada, the same is true under natural justice. In the United Kingdom, common law still requires a valid cause of action. In Australia, courts cannot proceed without justiciable controversy. The words differ, but the rule is the same. A claim without proof is void. A proceeding without cause is abuse.

When entering a courtroom, a sovereign does not behave with arrogance. You do not insult the judge, for that creates dishonour. You do not refuse to answer at all, for silence may be treated as consent. Instead, you stand and ask questions. You ask who is making a claim against you. You ask whether that man or woman will accept liability for fraud if their claim is false. You ask whether harm, loss, or fraud is alleged. These questions cut through procedure. They expose whether the proceeding is lawful or policy enforcement.

Many people fall into the trap of making declarations. They declare themselves sovereign, free, or beyond jurisdiction. Officials treat these declarations as nonsense, because they are delivered without context. Sovereignty is not proven by declaration. It is proven by conduct. You do not need to announce sovereignty. You live it by refusing dishonour and fraud. You stand calmly, ask questions, and make remedy if you have erred.

Outside the courtroom, encounters with authority are often less formal but no less important. A council officer may knock demanding payment. A police officer may question you in the street. A regulatory agent may call at your business. In every case, the same method applies. Do not argue. Do not submit blindly. Ask questions, remain peaceful, and preserve honour.

For example, when approached by a police officer in the United States who asks for identification, the sovereign asks whether they are obliged to provide it. In some states, only if you are suspected of a crime must you give your name. In Canada, outside of driving or alcohol laws, there is no general obligation to identify unless under arrest. In the United Kingdom, police may demand name and address only in specific circumstances defined by statute. In Australia, requirements differ by state, but always depend on suspicion of offence. By asking calmly, you prevent unlawful overreach.

Another example is taxation. In all four nations, tax agencies rely heavily on voluntary compliance. They send notices that appear mandatory, but they are offers for you to declare liability. When challenged to prove that liability exists in law, agencies often avoid clear answers. A sovereign does not ignore notices, for silence can be taken as consent. You respond with questions. You ask whether the agency can show contract. You ask whether they can show harm or loss. You ask who will take liability if their demand is false. Such responses keep you in honour and expose presumption.

Encounters with authority also test your ability to remain free of anger. It is easy to shout when threatened. It is easy to mock officials or insult them. But this is dishonour. It harms peace and gives officials justification to act harshly. Strength lies in calmness. If you are arrested, you remain silent except for peaceful questions. If you are fined, you request proof of claim. If you are threatened, you ask for liability in writing. These acts do not prevent all hardship, but they preserve honour and set record.

In America, many men and women have prevailed in court simply by refusing to step into dishonour. In Canada, ordinary people have halted administrative overreach by asking steady questions. In the United Kingdom, persistent honourable challenge has exposed unlawful council practices. In Australia, men and women who refused to be intimidated have forced agencies to retreat. These outcomes were not won by shouting or resisting physically. They were won by peace, patience, and clarity.

Preparation is vital. You cannot wait until an encounter to decide how to act. Rehearse your responses. Write down the questions you will ask. Practise keeping your voice calm. Remember that fear is the weapon of authority. When fear is removed, power dissolves.

Another principle is witness. If possible, record encounters. In America, courts have upheld the right to record police in public. In Canada, citizens are free to record officials so long as they are party to the conversation. In the United Kingdom, recording is lawful in most encounters. In Australia, laws vary by state, but one party consent is common. Recording preserves truth. Officials behave differently when they know they are being observed. Your speech remains careful when you know it is on record.

Encounters with authority will always carry risk. You may be fined, arrested, or punished despite honourable conduct. Sovereignty does not guarantee immunity. What it guarantees is peace within yourself. You know you have not lied. You know you have not harmed. You know you have not deceived. That peace is stronger than any penalty. In the long run, truth prevails. Systems built on fear collapse, but honour endures.

At the end of this chapter, remember that authority is only lawful when it aligns with the maxims. If an official prevents harm, loss, or fraud, they act in honour. If they exceed this, they act in policy. Your duty is not to fight them but to remain sovereign. You stand, you ask, you remain peaceful. That is all. This is the way encounters with authority become opportunities to show who you are, not traps to make you dishonour yourself.

Chapter 4
Property and Possessions

The question of property lies at the heart of sovereignty. Who owns what, who controls use, and who bears the risk of loss are questions that shape every society. Governments claim power over property through taxation, regulation, and seizure. Banks claim power through mortgages, liens, and credit agreements. Corporations claim power through contracts and licences. Yet underneath these claims, the same simple maxim governs all: cause no loss. If property is taken without consent, loss has been caused. If possessions are damaged without remedy, harm has been done. If ownership is misrepresented, fraud has occurred.

From the earliest days of law, property was respected because it prevented conflict. A man who planted a field or built a home was recognised as having a right to the fruits of his labour. To trespass or take from him without agreement was dishonourable. In America, the Constitution recognises property as central, protecting against deprivation without due process. In Canada, property rights are less explicit but protected through common law. In the United Kingdom, centuries of cases show property as the backbone of commerce. In Australia, the Constitution restricts compulsory acquisition to cases where just terms are given. These systems are imperfect, but they admit the principle that property must be respected.

A sovereign man or woman does not look to the state for proof of ownership. Registration may exist, but possession and use in honour are stronger. If you build, grow, or exchange in fairness, the property is yours by natural right. The state may register it, tax it, or attempt to seize it, but the maxim remains. If they take without proof of harm or loss, they act dishonourably. That dishonour may be hidden under statutes, yet it remains dishonour in truth.

Possessions carry duties as well as rights. To respect your neighbour's goods is as important as defending your own. If you borrow and fail to return, you cause loss. If you damage and deny it, you commit fraud. If you misuse and harm another's enjoyment, you cause harm. Remedy is simple: return, replace, repair. This requires no statute. Children learn it before they can read. Yet adults forget it when distracted by contracts, insurances, and policies. Sovereignty brings you back to basics.

Consider a simple example. A neighbour lends you a ladder. You forget to return it. Weeks pass. The neighbour suffers loss because they cannot use what is theirs. No law code is needed to see the dishonour. Remedy is to return the ladder promptly or provide a new one. If you deny having borrowed it, you have compounded loss with fraud. This is how disputes grow into lawsuits. A sovereign does not let such matters escalate. You admit the truth and make remedy.

In commerce, property questions often arise around payment. If you take goods without paying, you cause loss. If you promise to pay later and never do, you commit fraud. If you return damaged goods and deny responsibility, you cause harm. In every jurisdiction, such acts are unlawful, but more importantly, they are dishonourable. Sovereigns know that their word in trade must be as strong as their word in speech. To buy without means to pay is deceit. To sell without delivering is fraud. To promise service and not perform is loss.

Governments complicate property by claiming ownership of land and demanding tribute. In the United States, property tax means you never fully own your land, for failure to pay leads to seizure. In Canada, the same system exists through municipal taxation. In the United Kingdom, council tax and rates act as a form of rent to the state. In Australia, land tax and rates achieve the same result. These claims rest on presumption that the state is ultimate owner. Yet the maxim still stands. If a man or woman holds land in peace, harms none, causes no loss, and commits no fraud, what lawful claim exists against them? The state may act with power, but power without harm, loss, or fraud is not honour.

Another area of conflict is repossession. Banks claim property when loans are not repaid. They rely on contracts filled with complex terms. Yet if fraud is present in the creation of the contract, the claim is void. In America, foreclosure crises revealed massive fraud in mortgage documents. In Canada, banks have been caught misrepresenting terms. In the United Kingdom, hidden commissions in finance agreements have been exposed. In Australia, unfair lending practices have been challenged. In each case, fraud undermined the bank's claim. A sovereign challenges such claims not with violence but with questions. Was full disclosure given? Were the terms clear? Was consent real? If not, the contract is dishonourable.

Property disputes also arise between neighbours. Boundaries may be unclear. Trees may grow across lines. Water may flow from one to another. In such cases, the sovereign approach is dialogue, not litigation. Ask whether harm has been caused. Ask whether loss is real. Ask whether fraud is present. Most disputes dissolve when these questions are asked openly. If harm or loss is real, agree to remedy it. If none exists, let the matter rest. Courts escalate disputes by assigning blame and imposing penalties. Sovereigns resolve disputes by making peace.

Possessions also include the tools of life: vehicles, phones, clothing, and more. Governments impose licences and registrations, claiming that you must have permission to use your own goods. In America, driving requires a licence. In Canada, the same. In the United Kingdom and Australia, similar systems exist. Yet a vehicle is property. To use it in peace, causing no harm, loss, or fraud, is your natural right. Licensing assumes you are engaged in commerce or danger. A sovereign asks the simple question: who is harmed by my peaceful use? If no one, then no lawful claim exists. Officials may still enforce policy, but dishonour remains theirs, not yours.

Property is also bound up with inheritance. Families often fight when possessions are passed from one generation to another. States intervene with taxes and rules. But the maxim remains. If a man leaves his goods to his children, honour requires that his will be respected. To contest it without cause is to cause loss. To forge documents is to commit fraud. To seize before rightful time is to cause harm. Sovereigns respect the wishes of the departed and honour agreements made in family.

Across America, Canada, the United Kingdom, and Australia, property law has been buried under complexity. Yet underneath, the principle is unchanged. Ownership comes from honest acquisition and peaceful use. Loss comes from theft, damage, or deceit. Fraud destroys all claims. Sovereignty strips away the complexity and restores clarity. You respect what is yours and defend it with honour. You respect what is another's and never take it without agreement.

Property also extends beyond physical goods. Reputation, privacy, and creative works are possessions too. When a man spreads lies about another, he robs him of reputation. When a government spies without consent, it takes privacy. When a corporation copies the work of a creator without agreement, it commits theft of labour. In every jurisdiction, laws exist to address these matters, but the maxims explain them in plain truth. False words that harm reputation are fraud. Unwanted surveillance is harm. Theft of creation is loss. Sovereignty teaches you to respect these invisible possessions as much as physical ones.

Consider the matter of debt. A bank lends credit created from signatures and then claims repayment with interest. If the borrower knew the truth, there would be no fraud. But if the bank hides it, fraud is committed. In the United States, countless court cases have shown fraudulent lending. In Canada, predatory lending has been exposed. In the United Kingdom, secret commissions in finance agreements have been judged unlawful. In Australia, unfair contracts legislation acknowledges the imbalance. The common thread is deceit. Fraud in property dealings poisons the entire exchange. Sovereignty means refusing to be party to such fraud and demanding remedy when it occurs.

Possessions are also tested in times of crisis. Natural disasters, wars, or financial collapses often lead governments to seize goods or restrict use. During emergencies, officials justify taking food, fuel, or homes. Yet if no harm, loss, or fraud exists, what lawful claim do they have? Power is not the same as law. The sovereign recognises that emergency does not cancel maxims. To take property without consent or remedy is dishonour, regardless of excuse.

A man or woman living in sovereignty also respects common use. Some resources belong to all: air, rivers, forests, and oceans. To pollute them is to cause loss to the community. To hoard them unjustly is to cause harm. In America, environmental disputes often turn on proof of harm. In Canada, indigenous claims rest on loss of traditional use. In the United Kingdom, common rights are centuries old. In Australia, water rights have been the subject of bitter conflict. These disputes show that possessions can be individual or shared, but the maxim still applies. Use what is yours without destroying what belongs to others.

Governments often use property as a tool of control. Fines, fees, and confiscations act as punishment. Yet punishment without harm, loss, or fraud is not lawful. To seize a car for non-payment of tax is theft by another name. To confiscate goods for lack of licence is dishonour. To freeze bank accounts without evidence is fraud. Across America, Canada, the United Kingdom, and Australia, civil forfeiture laws have been abused in this way. The sovereign response is to demand proof of lawful claim, not to resist violently but to challenge fraud with truth.

Possessions are also tied to labour. Your time, your skill, your energy are your property. To compel work without fair pay is loss. To deceive workers with false promises is fraud. To harm them through unsafe conditions is injury. This is why labour disputes across all nations centre on fairness. Sovereigns recognise that wages are not charity. They are exchange for property in the form of labour. To cheat in that exchange is dishonourable.

Family disputes over possessions show the same pattern. Brothers may quarrel over inheritance. Parents may argue over gifts. Children may feel entitled. Yet the maxim brings clarity. Who acquired it in peace? Who holds it in truth? Who causes loss by taking without consent? Fraud and harm must be excluded. Remedy may be painful but it is simple. Agree, restore, move on. Sovereigns do not allow possessions to destroy relationships.

Consider also technology. Digital possessions are new but bound by old principles. A password is property. A file is property. To steal or corrupt them is loss. To copy without consent is fraud. In America, copyright law is vast, yet the maxim is simple. In Canada, fair dealing balances use and respect. In the United Kingdom, intellectual property rights protect creation. In Australia, similar protections exist. But the sovereign need not memorise statutes. You only need to ask whether taking another's creation without consent causes loss. If it does, remedy is required.

Another dimension is communal property. Town halls, roads, and parks are shared by all. Governments claim management, but the people remain owners. When such property is misused or neglected, the community suffers loss. Sovereigns act as caretakers, not vandals. To damage shared goods is to harm neighbours. To steal from the commons is to defraud the community. Respect for shared possessions is as vital as respect for private ones.

Property disputes also highlight the importance of witnesses. In early common law, property transfers were often witnessed by neighbours to prevent fraud. In America, deeds are notarised. In Canada, affidavits serve similar roles. In the United Kingdom, land registries record transfers. In Australia, titles are recorded under Torrens systems. Yet at the core, witnesses simply affirm truth. Fraud becomes harder when others stand to confirm honesty. Sovereigns rely on witnesses not because the state requires it but because truth loves light.

It is also necessary to address trespass. To enter another's land without cause is harm. To remain when asked to leave is loss. To deceive to gain entry is fraud. In every jurisdiction, trespass is recognised as unlawful. Sovereignty accepts this not out of fear of statute but from respect. You would not want your possessions invaded. You extend the same courtesy. If entry is needed, you ask permission. If refused, you respect it. Honour preserves peace.

In closing, property and possessions are a mirror of sovereignty itself. They reflect how you treat others and how you expect to be treated. Governments and corporations complicate property for their own gain, but the maxims restore clarity. What you earn, build, or exchange in fairness is yours. What belongs to another must be respected. Taking without agreement causes loss. Damaging without remedy causes harm. Misrepresenting ownership is fraud. These truths apply in America, Canada, the United Kingdom, and Australia equally. They apply to land, goods, reputation, labour, and creation. They apply to families, neighbours, and communities.

To live as a sovereign is to live with clean hands regarding property. You defend what is yours without greed. You respect what is another's without envy. You share what is common without waste. When disputes arise, you seek remedy, not escalation. In this way, possessions become not a source of conflict but a ground for peace. A sovereign man or woman remembers always that honour is greater than ownership. To keep possessions in dishonour is to lose sovereignty. To hold them in honour is to strengthen freedom.

Chapter 5
Commerce and Work

Commerce is the exchange of value between men and women. Work is the labour by which we create value. Both are central to daily life. Without commerce, goods remain unused. Without work, there is nothing to exchange. Sovereignty requires that both commerce and work be conducted in honour. Every trade, every contract, every wage agreement must align with the maxims. If loss is caused, if fraud is committed, if harm results, the exchange is dishonourable.

In ancient times, commerce was simple. A man traded grain for tools. A woman exchanged cloth for food. Work was offered, value was returned, and both walked away satisfied. Honour was preserved when promises were kept and goods were fair. Dishonour arose when one side cheated, withheld, or lied. These principles have not changed, though today commerce is layered with contracts, taxes, and regulations. The sovereign strips away the layers and asks the same questions. Was there harm, loss, or fraud? If so, remedy is required. If not, peace is preserved.

In the United States, contract law is built upon offer, acceptance, and consideration. The same in Canada, where courts require a meeting of minds. In the United Kingdom, centuries of cases affirm that a contract must be clear and fair. In Australia, courts enforce agreements only when terms are certain and consent is genuine. Across all jurisdictions, the same truths emerge. Fraud voids a contract. Loss demands remedy. Harm calls for restoration. A sovereign does not need to memorise all the statutes. The maxims already hold the answers.

Work is a form of property. Your time, skill, and energy belong to you. When you offer them in exchange for wages or goods, you are trading property. To underpay or deceive a worker is theft. To demand labour without consent is slavery. To endanger workers is harm. In America, labour law grew from struggles against exploitation. In Canada, similar protections developed through union battles. In the United Kingdom, child labour laws and factory reforms admitted that exploitation was loss and harm. In Australia, unfair dismissal and workplace safety laws reflect the same principles. These laws are imperfect reflections of the maxims, but the maxims themselves are enough.

A sovereign man or woman approaches work with clarity. You state clearly what you will provide. You ask clearly what you will receive. You keep your word, and you expect the same in return. If the exchange is unequal, you address it peacefully. If fraud is attempted, you expose it. If harm is threatened, you refuse it. This is honour.

Commerce in the modern age is heavily burdened by intermediaries. Banks, tax agencies, and regulators insert themselves into every exchange. They demand a portion of value, though they provide no labour. In America, income tax is withheld from wages before the worker touches it. In Canada, similar systems apply. In the United Kingdom, PAYE takes earnings at source. In Australia, PAYG serves the same role. These systems presume that the state owns a share of your labour. The sovereign questions this presumption. If no harm, loss, or fraud has been caused, what lawful claim exists?

Fraud in commerce is common. Advertising promises what products cannot deliver. Contracts hide unfair terms in fine print. Credit agreements deceive borrowers with unclear interest. Governments impose fees as though they are lawful obligations. In every case, dishonour is present. A sovereign does not rage at these systems but navigates them with awareness. You read carefully. You question politely. You refuse to consent blindly. Fraud only succeeds when men and women accept it without challenge.

Work itself must be honourable. To take pay without working is fraud. To waste time while claiming labour is theft. To deceive an employer about skill or effort is dishonour. A sovereign does not excuse laziness or deceit by pointing to corruption at the top. You keep your side clean even if others do not. Honour is not conditional. It is a duty.

Commerce also includes barter, trade, and informal exchange. These occur outside official systems yet remain bound by the maxims. If you trade one good for another, both must be as promised. If you sell food, it must be safe. If you exchange labour, it must be performed. Fraud poisons even small exchanges. A sovereign keeps promises regardless of scale.

Disputes in commerce often arise from unclear terms. One party expects more than the other agreed to provide. This is why clarity is essential. In America, courts enforce contracts only when terms are definite. In Canada, ambiguity weakens enforcement. In the United Kingdom and Australia, vagueness leads to disputes. The sovereign avoids this by speaking plainly, writing clearly, and ensuring both sides understand. When both know the terms, peace follows.

Governments often regulate commerce under the claim of protecting fairness. Consumer laws, trade regulations, and licensing are presented as safeguards. Yet these systems often serve the state more than the people. They create dependency and confusion. The sovereign relies instead on the maxims. You know that if harm, loss, or fraud is avoided, the exchange is lawful. You do not need endless regulation to tell you what is fair.

Another area of dishonour in commerce is monopolies and coercion. When corporations dominate markets, they limit choice and inflate prices. This causes loss to the people. In America, antitrust law arose to address such abuse. In Canada, competition law serves the same purpose. In the United Kingdom and Australia, competition authorities claim to preserve fairness. Yet dishonour remains because enforcement is selective. The sovereign sees through appearances. Any system that limits choice and forces terms causes loss. You respond by seeking alternatives, supporting fair trade, and building community exchanges.

Work is also dishonoured when men and women surrender their labour for benefits rather than standing in honour. Welfare systems across all nations create dependence. They provide survival at the cost of sovereignty. Fraud is common, with claims made dishonestly or benefits taken without need. This dishonour weakens both the individual and the community. A sovereign accepts help when in true need but never treats dependence as a way of life. Work, however humble, restores honour.

Commerce between nations illustrates the same truths. When one nation exploits another through unfair trade, it causes loss. When corporations plunder resources without consent, they commit fraud. When wars are fought for profit, they cause mass harm. Sovereignty teaches that honour in trade must extend beyond borders. Men and women are not free if their wealth comes from the suffering of others.

Commerce and work therefore are not separate from sovereignty but central to it. How you earn, how you spend, how you trade reveals your honour. Fraud, loss, and harm in these areas poison life. Honour in these areas strengthens freedom. A sovereign lives by the maxims not only in courts and encounters with officials but in every exchange of value.

Commerce is often weaponised through debt. Credit cards, loans, and mortgages appear to offer opportunity but in truth are chains. A man signs thinking he borrows value, yet the bank creates numbers from nothing. He labours for years to repay what never truly existed. This is fraud at the highest level. In the United States, credit card debt enslaves millions. In Canada, household debt is among the highest in the world. In the United Kingdom, payday lenders preyed on the poor until scandals exposed their tricks. In Australia, banking royal commissions revealed systemic fraud. These stories all show that dishonour in commerce breeds misery. The sovereign recognises the fraud, asks questions, and refuses to bind himself to deceit.

Work too can be corrupted when men and women surrender dignity for survival. Employers exploit desperation, paying less than agreed, demanding hours without rest, or ignoring safety. This causes loss and harm. Governments claim to regulate workplaces, but enforcement is patchy. Sovereignty means taking responsibility to protect your own labour. You refuse to work under terms that destroy your honour. You seek remedy when cheated. You expose fraud when it appears. Even if the system fails, you remain clean.

In America, wage theft is rampant. In Canada, migrant workers are often exploited. In the United Kingdom, zero hour contracts have been criticised for dishonour. In Australia, underpayment scandals in large corporations show the same pattern. These are not accidents but systems of fraud. A sovereign does not excuse them. You either demand remedy or withdraw your labour. By doing so you show that your work is property, not a resource for others to plunder.

Commerce also teaches patience and discernment. Temptation to profit dishonourably is strong. You may be offered a chance to cheat a customer, to hide defects, to mislead in advertising. These offers test your honour. If you accept, you gain short profit but lose sovereignty. If you refuse, you may lose money but keep peace. Sovereigns choose peace. Profit built on fraud is a chain. Wealth built on honour is freedom.

Work in community demonstrates this clearly. A builder who cuts corners causes harm. A doctor who withholds truth causes loss. A teacher who lies to children commits fraud. In each case, dishonour poisons the profession. Sovereignty in work means offering labour as service, not exploitation. You provide value honestly. You speak truth about limits. You repair mistakes. In this way your work becomes a mirror of the maxims.

Commerce also includes how you use money itself. Hoarding while others suffer may not be fraud, but it can cause loss. Spending recklessly may harm your family. Investing in dishonourable ventures spreads fraud. A sovereign considers the effect of money choices. Does this exchange cause harm? Does it inflict loss on others? Is there deceit in it? If yes, it is avoided. If no, it may be pursued. This approach applies in every jurisdiction and in every form of trade.

Modern systems push men and women to separate work from meaning. Jobs are offered as survival, not service. People work for wages while hating their labour. This is dishonour, for it devalues time and skill. Sovereignty means seeking work that aligns with peace. Even humble tasks can be honourable if done with truth and care. Dishonourable work, no matter the pay, erodes freedom.

In America, many men and women have left corporate jobs to build small businesses that honour their values. In Canada, community co-operatives thrive on fair exchange. In the United Kingdom, local markets and skill shares reflect old traditions of honourable trade. In Australia, barter and local exchange networks allow work without government interference. These examples show that sovereignty in commerce and work is possible when men and women choose maxims over profit.

It is also necessary to address corruption in governments themselves. Officials often take bribes, award contracts to friends, or use public money for private gain. This is fraud on a vast scale. It causes loss to every taxpayer and harm to public trust. Sovereigns cannot control every instance of corruption, but they can refuse to imitate it. You cannot expose dishonour at the top if you excuse it in yourself. By living in honour at the level of your own commerce and work, you weaken the spread of fraud.

Some men and women attempt to escape dishonour in commerce by withdrawing entirely. They avoid jobs, markets, and trade. But isolation is not sovereignty. To live in community requires exchange. The answer is not withdrawal but clean conduct. Engage in commerce, but do so honourably. Work in society, but keep your word. Refuse fraud, repair loss, prevent harm. In this way you show others a better path without leaving the world.

Commerce and work also link to future generations. Children watch how parents trade and labour. If they see lies and shortcuts, they learn dishonour. If they see honesty and remedy, they learn sovereignty. Every meal bought, every wage earned, every service provided is a lesson. Sovereignty is taught not by speeches but by daily exchanges.

In the end, commerce and work reveal the heart of the maxims. Do no harm means you do not endanger others with your products or services. Cause no loss means you provide fair value for fair value. Commit no fraud means your words and contracts are true. These three principles are simple, but they cover the whole of commerce and work. Statutes may try to regulate every detail, but they are unnecessary when honour is present.

Across America, Canada, the United Kingdom, and Australia, the systems of commerce are tangled. Taxes are high, debt is deep, fraud is common. Yet men and women who live by the maxims cut through the tangle. You stand in truth, work with honour, and trade in fairness. In doing so, you reclaim sovereignty over the most basic part of life: the exchange of value.

The sovereign knows that labour is sacred, commerce is natural, and honour is required. Without these, life is slavery. With them, life is free.

Chapter 6
Community Dealings

No man or woman lives entirely alone. Even the most independent sovereign depends on neighbours, tradesmen, and family. Community is the network of daily dealings through which we share space and resources. How you conduct yourself in this network determines whether peace or conflict will rule your life. A sovereign man or woman recognises that the same maxims that govern speech, property, and commerce also govern community. When you meet your neighbour, when you settle disputes, when you join in common projects, you must remember to do no harm, cause no loss, and commit no fraud.

Community dealings are often where sovereignty is most tested. With officials, the path is clearer: demand proof, ask questions, avoid dishonour. With neighbours, disputes are personal. Emotion runs high. Pride interferes with honour. Yet it is here that sovereignty must be lived most carefully. If you cannot live in peace with those next to you, how will you stand before the state?

Across all nations, local disputes often end in courts. In America, small claims courts are filled with neighbours arguing over fences, noise, and pets. In Canada, landlord and tenant boards hear endless quarrels. In the United Kingdom, magistrates are burdened with minor community offences. In Australia, tribunals resolve disputes about trees, boundaries, and shared property. Yet these disputes need not reach officials. The maxims offer a simpler, more peaceful solution.

Imagine two neighbours disputing a tree. One says the branches drop leaves on his roof, causing cost and labour. The other says the tree provides shade and beauty. The question is whether harm, loss, or fraud is present. Has damage been caused? Has property been lost? Has deceit been involved? If so, remedy is required. If not, the matter should rest. Honour demands dialogue before escalation. Sovereigns call for remedy, not punishment.

Fraud is particularly destructive in community. When a man lies about his neighbour, spreading false stories, he poisons trust. When a woman misrepresents her dealings, she divides families. Fraud in community leads to harm and loss far beyond money. It breaks peace. That is why every culture punishes fraud harshly. In America, defamation suits seek to restore reputation. In Canada, truth is a full defence but lies bring remedy. In the United Kingdom, libel has been treated as a serious wrong for centuries. In Australia, defamation cases are common and damages significant. The principle is always the same: truth preserves peace, lies destroy it.

Community dealings also include shared resources. A well, a road, a hall, or a field may be used by all. To misuse these is to harm the whole. To exploit them selfishly is to cause loss. To claim ownership falsely is fraud. Sovereigns treat shared property with respect. In America, town commons once provided grazing for all. In Canada, community forests and fisheries are governed by custom. In the United Kingdom, ancient rights of way preserve shared access. In Australia, indigenous traditions emphasise collective use of land and water. All reflect the same truth: shared resources require shared honour.

When disputes arise, remedy is the sovereign path. Remedy does not mean punishment but restoration. If harm is caused, it is repaired. If loss is inflicted, it is replaced. If fraud is committed, truth is spoken and peace restored. This is different from punishment, which seeks revenge. Sovereigns do not seek revenge. They seek peace. In America, restorative justice programmes show this principle in practice. In Canada, community mediation is common. In the United Kingdom, alternative dispute resolution resolves matters outside court. In Australia, local councils offer mediation to preserve harmony. These are institutional reflections of the maxims. Sovereigns live them daily without waiting for officials.

Community also involves commerce on a small scale. Buying eggs from a neighbour, lending tools, helping with repairs. Each of these is a contract of trust. Fraud or loss in such dealings poisons relationships. To take without giving, to borrow without returning, to promise without performing, all create dishonour. Sovereignty requires strict honesty in small dealings. A man who cheats in little matters cannot stand in big ones.

Another test of sovereignty is gossip. Words spoken in community spread fast. To repeat rumours without proof can cause great harm. To invent stories is outright fraud. A sovereign speaks truth or remains silent. If you hear dishonour spoken, you challenge it gently. You ask whether proof exists. You defend the absent if they are falsely accused. This preserves peace. In every jurisdiction, courts recognise slander as unlawful. Sovereigns know it is dishonour even when no court is involved.

Community also involves service. Men and women who contribute to the whole gain trust. Those who take without giving lose it. In America, volunteers keep towns alive. In Canada, service groups maintain strength. In the United Kingdom, village committees organise common life. In Australia, local clubs build bonds. Sovereigns understand that giving service without expectation strengthens community and protects sovereignty. When you help others, they defend your honour in return.

Conflicts will always arise in community, but they need not become battles. The sovereign seeks dialogue, asks questions, and restores peace. Courts may escalate, but neighbours can settle. You do not need statutes to know when to cut a tree, mend a fence, or share a path. You need only the maxims. Do no harm. Cause no loss. Commit no fraud. Applied with patience, these are enough to live in peace with those around you.

Community also reveals how quickly dishonour spreads if not checked. One false claim, one broken promise, one unfair taking can poison relations for years. Families divide, neighbours quarrel, and entire towns are marked by bitterness. Courts are full of such cases. Yet every one of them could have been prevented if the maxims had been honoured at the first step. When you do no harm, cause no loss, and commit no fraud, disputes fade before they grow.

The challenge is that pride often prevents remedy. A man who has caused loss may deny it out of fear of shame. A woman who has spoken falsehood may double down rather than admit it. Pride becomes fraud, and fraud deepens loss. The sovereign refuses this path. You admit fault quickly, you restore what is missing, and you speak truth even when painful. By doing so you prevent dishonour from spreading through the community.

Consider the matter of boundaries. Across America, Canada, the United Kingdom, and Australia, disputes about land borders are common. A fence built slightly over the line, a hedge trimmed too far, or a driveway extended without consent can spark conflict. Courts may take years to decide such cases. Yet the maxim provides an answer at once. If harm has been caused, remedy it. If loss has occurred, restore it. If fraud has been attempted, confess and correct it. Sovereigns resolve such matters directly with neighbours, sparing both the expense and the dishonour of litigation.

Noise and nuisance are another test. A man plays music late at night, disturbing his neighbours. A dog barks constantly, keeping the street awake. These are not great crimes, but they are harm. Honour requires that the offender admit it and change behaviour. Officials may write bylaws and issue fines, but sovereigns rely on dialogue. Speak directly, explain the harm, and agree on remedy. This preserves peace and builds respect.

Shared projects also test honour. Communities often join to build halls, repair roads, or maintain parks. Each member promises labour or materials. Fraud enters when promises are broken or resources misused. Loss is caused when some carry more than their share. Harm is caused when resentment grows. The sovereign ensures clarity at the start. What will each provide? What remedy will follow if they fail? By speaking openly, you prevent dishonour. This is how free men and women govern themselves without endless statutes.

Community also shows the danger of envy. To covet another's goods, to resent their success, is dishonour. Envy leads to false accusations, theft, and harm. Sovereigns guard against envy by remembering that property gained in honour is sacred. You celebrate your neighbour's success, for it harms you not. If loss comes, you address it truthfully. Envy is fraud against the heart. It deceives you into seeing harm where none exists.

Across the nations, community traditions have long provided models of honour. In America, town meetings once governed by direct agreement. In Canada, indigenous councils emphasised consensus and remedy. In the United Kingdom, parish life depended on mutual service. In Australia, local communities long relied on sharing and witness. These traditions worked because men and women honoured the maxims. Where dishonour entered, conflict followed.

Modern systems often replace community remedy with bureaucracy. Instead of neighbours resolving disputes, councils impose fines. Instead of families settling issues, courts dictate outcomes. This weakens responsibility and fosters dependence. The sovereign resists this by living remedy directly. You do not need a judge to tell you to repair damage you caused. You do not need a council officer to order you to respect your neighbour. Honour is enough.

Technology adds new challenges to community dealings. Social media allows gossip and fraud to spread quickly. A false story can harm reputation across the world in hours. Sovereigns must apply the same discipline online as in person. Speak truth, avoid harm, and never deceive. If you err, correct swiftly. Online communities are still communities. The maxims apply there as much as on the street.

Another challenge is multicultural living. In America, Canada, the United Kingdom, and Australia, communities contain many traditions, beliefs, and values. Sovereignty does not mean imposing your way on others. It means finding common ground in the maxims. Every culture values honesty. Every tradition condemns theft. Every people recognises harm. By focusing on these shared truths, communities of difference can live in peace. Sovereignty provides the bridge.

When officials intervene in community matters, sovereigns still stand in honour. If a dispute escalates to council or court, you present truth calmly. You admit what is yours, deny what is not, and offer remedy where due. You do not argue endlessly. You do not defame your neighbour. You show honour even under pressure. By doing so you preserve sovereignty even when the system intrudes.

Community dealings also involve teaching. Children learn how to live by watching how adults treat each other. If they see gossip, envy, and dishonour, they repeat them. If they see remedy, honesty, and peace, they repeat those instead. The sovereign therefore has duty not only to act rightly but to model it. Every dispute settled in peace is a lesson. Every promise kept is instruction. Sovereignty grows when it is shown, not only spoken.

In conclusion, community is where sovereignty is most visible. It is easy to talk of freedom in theory. It is harder to live it when your neighbour's dog keeps you awake or when a shared fence needs repair. Yet these small matters reveal your honour more than grand speeches. If you live the maxims here, you will live them anywhere. If you fail here, no declaration will save you in greater trials.

The sovereign man or woman therefore treats every community dealing as sacred. You do not cause harm. You do not inflict loss. You do not spread fraud. You admit when you fail and make remedy. You respect shared resources and private property alike. You live in peace with neighbours, family, and strangers. By doing so you strengthen not only yourself but the whole community. Honour spreads as surely as dishonour. When you live by the maxims, you draw others into peace. This is how sovereignty moves from the individual to the world.

Chapter 7
Truth in Record

Every system of law depends on records. Without records, no claim could be proved, no right defended, no contract enforced. A record is simply a testimony preserved, whether on paper, stone, or digital file. For this reason, records are powerful. They shape memory, guide courts, and direct governments. Yet because they carry power, they also attract fraud. To corrupt a record is to poison truth itself.

Sovereignty requires truth in record. A man or woman who speaks honourably but signs dishonourably is divided. A man who stands in peace but files false documents is dishonest. Sovereigns do not live double lives. Your speech, your contracts, your notices, and your affidavits must be true. Fraud in record is still fraud, even if no one sees it but you.

From the earliest times, oaths on record were treated as sacred. In America, the Constitution demands oaths of office, binding officials to honour. In Canada, oaths of allegiance are required in courts and parliaments. In the United Kingdom, sworn affidavits underpin justice. In Australia, statutory declarations serve the same purpose. All are attempts to secure truth in record. Yet the sovereign does not rely on ceremony. You know that every word you place on record binds you. Whether notarised or not, whether stamped or not, your word in writing is your honour.

Fraud in record is a common tool of control. Governments record you at birth, creating a paper identity. Banks record debts, claiming obligations that were never fully disclosed. Corporations record contracts with terms hidden in small print. Courts record judgments that do not reflect true harm or loss. All of these are records, yet many are fraudulent. The sovereign response is not to ignore records but to challenge them with truth. If a record misrepresents you, you correct it. If a record binds you falsely, you rebut it. If a record accuses you without evidence, you demand proof.

The importance of record can be seen in property disputes. In America, title deeds determine ownership, yet fraudulent deeds have stolen homes. In Canada, land registries are trusted, yet errors occur. In the United Kingdom, title records can be altered without consent. In Australia, the Torrens system records ownership, but fraud has still been committed. These systems admit the power of record but also reveal its vulnerability. The maxim reminds you that fraud destroys everything. A fraudulent record, no matter how official, is void in truth.

Records also matter in finance. When you sign a loan agreement, you place yourself on record. If the terms are fraudulent, the agreement is dishonourable. Yet once signed, it is presumed valid until challenged. Sovereigns know that signature is not a casual act. It is record. You sign only what is true. You do not allow fear or haste to trick you. In America, courts presume a signed contract reflects consent. In Canada, signatures bind unless fraud is shown. In the United Kingdom and Australia, the same rule applies. Your protection is not law but honour. Refuse to sign what is false.

Truth in record also means accuracy in your own dealings. If you send a notice, it must be true. If you file an affidavit, it must be honest. If you testify, it must reflect your knowledge. Fraudulent notices and false claims dishonour the sender. Some who call themselves sovereign have filed wild documents, threatening officials or claiming false rights. This behaviour brings disrepute and dishonour. Sovereignty is not about overwhelming officials with paper but standing in truth. A single honest affidavit carries more weight than a hundred fraudulent filings.

Consider how courts across jurisdictions treat false records. In America, perjury in affidavit is a crime. In Canada, false declarations carry penalty. In the United Kingdom, forgery is severely punished. In Australia, false statutory declarations can bring prison. These penalties reflect recognition that fraud in record strikes at the heart of justice. The sovereign does not need threat of punishment to know this. You honour record because your word is sacred.

Truth in record also protects you from false claims. If you document your dealings, if you keep receipts, if you send notices, you can show honour. When accused, you have record. In America, courts require documentary evidence. In Canada, records form the backbone of trials. In the United Kingdom and Australia, judges weigh paper heavily. Without record, it is one word against another. With record, truth is clearer. Sovereigns do not drown themselves in paperwork, but they keep enough record to protect honour.

Technology has made record both easier and more dangerous. Emails, texts, and digital files are records. Social media posts are records. What you write in haste can be used later against you. A sovereign remembers that every word written may be permanent. You do not write lies, insults, or threats, for they remain. You write truth, peace, and remedy, for they will defend you.

Records also play a role in family. Births, marriages, and deaths are recorded by the state. These records are used to claim authority. Yet beyond state systems, families also keep records. Family bibles once preserved names and dates. Communities recorded agreements in local books. Sovereigns revive this practice by keeping private records of agreements, notices, and remedies. These stand as proof independent of state systems.

Truth in record is also vital in commerce. A receipt proves exchange. An invoice proves agreement. A contract proves terms. Fraud in any of these is dishonour. To falsify accounts is to deceive. To overstate value is to defraud. To hide terms is to cause loss. Sovereigns do not rely on complexity. You keep records simple, true, and clear.

At its core, truth in record is the outward reflection of inward honour. To lie on paper is to lie in spirit. To misrepresent in writing is to cheat in life. Sovereignty allows no division. You are whole in speech, in deed, and in record. The maxims demand consistency.

Records can protect or enslave, depending on how they are created and used. The state relies on record to maintain control. Every licence, registration, and certificate is a record. At birth, your name is placed into a registry. That registry is then used to create contracts, obligations, and claims. The paper identity is managed by record, and most men and women treat that identity as themselves. This is the first fraud, the confusion between the living being and the record.

A sovereign never forgets that the record is not the man or woman. A piece of paper is not alive. A government file is not flesh and blood. When an official waves a record, you ask whether it reflects truth. If it does, you honour it. If it does not, you rebut it. Rebuttal is not anger or denial. It is correction. You simply state that the record is inaccurate and provide truth. If you remain silent, the false record stands. This is why officials depend on silence. They know that unrebutted record is presumed true.

In America, the Uniform Commercial Code acknowledges that unrebutted statements on record stand as truth. In Canada, affidavits not challenged are accepted as evidence. In the United Kingdom, courts treat unrebutted claims as admissions. In Australia, statutory declarations not contested are taken as proof. These systems reveal a key principle: record unchallenged becomes reality in law. The sovereign uses this not for fraud but for truth. You put your word on record and stand by it. If challenged, you defend it with evidence. If not challenged, it stands.

Dishonour arises when men and women abuse this principle. Some flood courts with documents filled with false claims. They hope officials will be too overwhelmed to respond, leaving fraud unrebutted. This is not sovereignty. It is dishonour. Fraud in record poisons the well for all. Sovereigns know that one true affidavit is stronger than a pile of lies. You do not seek to trick the system. You seek to stand in peace.

Another danger in record is assumption. Many contracts contain terms that presume agreement unless rejected. A letter may say that silence equals consent. A notice may say that failure to respond is acceptance. If you do nothing, the record binds you. Sovereignty requires vigilance. You must read carefully, respond timely, and rebut falsehoods. In every jurisdiction, silence is often treated as agreement in commerce. This is why officials rely on it. They send notices knowing most people will never answer. The sovereign refuses silence when honour requires speech.

Truth in record also means preserving your own dealings. Keep copies of letters sent, notices delivered, and receipts given. This is not paranoia but honour. If a dispute arises, you have record to show truth. In America, certified mail and notaries provide evidence. In Canada, registered post and commissioners for oaths serve similar roles. In the United Kingdom, affidavits and sworn statements hold weight. In Australia, statutory declarations and recorded delivery provide proof. These tools are available to all, but few use them wisely. Sovereigns know that honour without record may be doubted. Honour with record is undeniable.

Records are also spiritual in weight. To swear falsely is not only a crime in law but a wound to the soul. Every culture warns against false oaths. In scripture, in custom, in tradition, perjury is treated as among the worst sins. This is because false record destroys trust in community. If words on paper cannot be trusted, no society can stand. Sovereignty therefore is not only practical but spiritual. You live truth in record because to do otherwise is to damage your own conscience.

Consider how dishonourable governments rely on false records. In America, foreclosure fraud involved banks fabricating documents to seize homes. In Canada, cases of forged signatures have been exposed in lending. In the United Kingdom, false accounting by corporations has destroyed pensions. In Australia, banking inquiries revealed systemic misrepresentation. In each case, fraud in record caused harm and loss to millions. Courts may punish some offenders, but the system often protects them. The sovereign learns the lesson: never trust a record simply because it is official. Always ask whether it reflects truth.

Community dealings also depend on record. Agreements between neighbours, family inheritances, and business ventures all create record, whether written or remembered. Memory fades, but written word remains. To fail to record an agreement is to invite dispute. To record it falsely is fraud. Sovereigns prefer simple, clear agreements written in plain words. You do not need complex contracts. You need clarity, honesty, and witnesses. In every nation, simple agreements are enforceable if they reflect true meeting of minds.

Truth in record also applies to history. Governments rewrite records of the past to justify present control. In America, textbooks omit truths of corruption. In Canada, records of indigenous treatment were hidden. In the United Kingdom, archives are closed to conceal dishonour. In Australia, colonial records were altered or destroyed. Fraud in record distorts memory. Sovereigns respond by preserving true record. Families, communities, and individuals write their own history and guard it. By doing so, they protect future generations from deceit.

Technology has amplified both the risk and the power of record. Digital signatures, blockchain, and online files make record more permanent but also more vulnerable to control. A sovereign adapts by ensuring that even digital records reflect truth. You do not hide behind anonymity to defraud. You use technology to preserve honesty. Whether in email, text, or ledger, your word must remain consistent.

In disputes with officials, truth in record is often your strongest defence. If you send notices asking for proof, and officials fail to respond, their silence is record. If you place on record that you are a living man or woman and not a fiction, and no rebuttal comes, that stands. If you demand evidence of harm, loss, or fraud and none is provided, the record shows dishonour on their side. Sovereigns use this principle not to boast but to protect peace.

The principle of clean hands applies strongly here. Courts of equity in America, Canada, the United Kingdom, and Australia all insist that one who seeks remedy must come with clean hands. Fraudulent record stains the hands. If you attempt to gain remedy through deceit, your claim collapses. Sovereigns never forget this. You win not by tricks but by truth.

In closing, truth in record is the written reflection of the maxims. Do no harm means you do not harm others through false documents. Cause no loss means you do not deprive others by misrepresentation in writing. Commit no fraud means every notice, contract, and affidavit you issue is clean. Across all four nations, record is treated as evidence of truth. The sovereign ensures that record reflects actual truth, not deceit. In this way your honour is preserved in speech, in deed, and in record alike.

Chapter 8
Paperwork and Promises

Paperwork has become the lifeblood of governments, corporations, and courts. Every demand arrives on paper. Every right is claimed on a form. Every penalty is issued through documents. Paper is treated as if it rules over flesh and blood. Yet paper is only record of words, and words are only powerful when they carry truth. Sovereigns know that paperwork is not magic. It is simply a record of promises. If the promises are honourable, they stand. If they are fraudulent, they collapse.

From birth, paperwork surrounds men and women. A birth certificate creates a record. A school enrolment form binds a child into systems. A driver's licence is issued. A tax number is assigned. In America, the social security number follows from paperwork. In Canada, the social insurance number arises. In the United Kingdom, the national insurance number is linked to records. In Australia, the tax file number serves the same purpose. These documents are presented as proof of identity, yet they are only paperwork. They do not create the living man or woman. They create a paper entity, which the state treats as subject.

Promises are equally powerful. Every signature on a contract is a promise. Every oath in court is a promise. Every notice sent is a promise. To promise falsely is fraud. To promise without intent to perform is dishonour. Sovereignty means that your promises are as sacred as your speech. You do not sign what you do not mean. You do not swear to what you do not know. You do not agree to what you cannot perform.

The problem is that modern systems bury promises under layers of paperwork. Contracts are written in long clauses few can understand. Forms hide obligations in fine print. Governments create endless rules that presume consent through paperwork. A sovereign strips away the confusion. You ask whether the paperwork reflects a real promise. Did you consent knowingly? Were the terms clear? Was there full disclosure? If not, the paperwork is fraudulent.

In the United States, contract law demands meeting of minds. If terms are hidden, no true agreement exists. In Canada, courts strike down contracts that are unconscionable. In the United Kingdom, misrepresentation voids agreements. In Australia, unfair contracts legislation reflects the same principle. These systems all admit the truth: paperwork without honour is worthless. Fraud vitiates everything.

Sovereigns therefore approach paperwork with caution. You do not fear paper, but you do not worship it. You treat it as what it is: record of promises. If the promise is honourable, you honour it. If it is fraudulent, you rebut it. If it is unclear, you refuse it until clarified. This is how you remain sovereign in a world drowning in forms.

Officials rely on paperwork to bind men and women silently. They send notices of tax, fines, and penalties. Most recipients pay without question. Yet each notice is an offer. Unless backed by proof of harm, loss, or fraud, it is not lawful. A sovereign replies with questions. What is the basis of this obligation? Who is making the claim? Will they accept liability if their record is false? If answers are not given, the paperwork is dishonourable.

Promises in community also matter. A handshake, a spoken agreement, or a casual assurance are promises too. If you break them without remedy, you commit fraud. Sovereignty demands that your word be consistent in every setting. Whether in court, in family, or in trade, you honour your promises. If you fail, you admit and restore.

Paperwork also includes notices you send. Many sovereign men and women use notices to assert rights or challenge claims. This is lawful when done in truth. A notice is simply a statement of your position and a call for response. If you state truthfully, and no rebuttal comes, your notice stands. But dishonour arises when notices contain threats, lies, or impossible claims. Officials ignore such documents because they lack truth. Sovereigns write simply, clearly, and truthfully. One honest notice carries more power than pages of falsehood.

Consider debt collection. In America, collectors send letters demanding payment. In Canada, similar demands are common. In the United Kingdom and Australia, agencies threaten court. Each letter is paperwork, but not always lawful. A sovereign asks: is this my debt? Was full disclosure given? Can you prove harm or loss? Who will accept liability for fraud if the claim is false? If answers do not come, the paperwork collapses. The same applies to every demand: challenge dishonour with truth.

Promises also bind officials. When an officer swears to uphold law, that is a promise. When a judge takes an oath, that is a promise. When a politician makes an election pledge, that is a promise. Fraud enters when they break these promises without remedy. Sovereigns remind officials of their promises. You hold them accountable not by rage but by truth. You point to their oath and ask whether they are honouring it. This method is powerful, for it exposes dishonour in their own record.

Paperwork in courts shows the same pattern. Complaints, summonses, and judgments are all records of promises. They allege obligations or wrongdoing. The sovereign asks whether they reflect harm, loss, or fraud. If not, they are policy, not law. You do not ignore them blindly, but you challenge them honourably. You file notices, you demand proof, you rebut falsehoods. This is not defiance but peace. You stand in honour, refusing fraud.

The greatest danger in paperwork is assumption. Men and women assume that a stamped document must be lawful. They assume that a signature from an official proves truth. They assume that complex words cannot be challenged. These assumptions give power to fraud. A sovereign does not assume. You ask questions. You demand clarity. You refuse to accept paper as master over flesh.

Birth registration is a clear example. The paper certificate records an event, but governments treat it as creation of a legal entity. That entity is then bound by obligations you never knowingly accepted. In America, this paper is linked to taxation and benefits. In Canada, it is tied to identification systems. In the United Kingdom, it becomes the foundation for a national insurance number. In Australia, it is linked to tax and welfare. All are paperwork. None of them creates a living being. Sovereignty begins by recognising that paperwork is record, not reality.

Another example is licences. A driving licence, a business permit, a marriage certificate, all are paperwork. They record promises to abide by conditions. But governments use them as levers of control. They say that without the paper, your actions are unlawful. Yet if you drive in peace, harm no one, and cause no loss, what claim exists against you? The paper does not create your right to travel, trade, or unite with another. It only records the event. Fraud enters when officials claim that paper is master.

Promises work the same way. If you make a promise you cannot keep, you commit fraud. If you sign a contract knowing you will not perform, you dishonour yourself. In America, fraud in inducement voids agreements. In Canada, misrepresentation does the same. In the United Kingdom, contracts without good faith collapse. In Australia, agreements gained through deceit are unenforceable. Every jurisdiction admits the same truth: a promise without honour is worthless.

Sovereigns treat every promise as sacred. You do not overstate your ability. You do not agree under pressure without reflection. You do not sign what you do not understand. If you cannot perform, you admit it and seek remedy. By doing this, you protect yourself and others from fraud. Your honour becomes visible in your dealings. Others learn that your promise can be trusted, even when systems fail.

Paperwork can also be a tool of remedy. When you send a notice of truth, you are placing your word on record. If the other side does not respond, your truth stands unrebutted. This is not trickery but procedure. In America, unrebutted affidavits are treated as evidence. In Canada, silence in the face of sworn testimony carries weight. In the United Kingdom and Australia, similar rules apply. Sovereigns use this principle carefully, never to deceive, always to uphold truth.

There is temptation to misuse paperwork. Some who call themselves sovereign file documents filled with threats, false claims, or invented laws. They hope to frighten officials or avoid obligations. This path is dishonour. Fraud in paperwork undermines sovereignty itself. It damages reputation and harms the wider movement. True sovereignty relies on clean record, not false intimidation.

When you receive paperwork from officials, you must respond in honour. To ignore completely is to risk presumption of consent. To argue angrily is to show dishonour. The sovereign path is to ask questions and demand proof. You state your position calmly. You require evidence of harm, loss, or fraud. If none is shown, you remain free. This method works across borders. In America, due process demands answer. In Canada, fairness requires disclosure. In the United Kingdom, proof is required for valid claim. In Australia, the same principle applies. Silence from officials exposes dishonour on their side, not yours.

Promises also extend into family life. Marriage, parenthood, and kinship all rest on promises. To break them dishonourably is to cause harm. Sovereignty requires faithfulness in these areas. You may fail, but you must admit and remedy. Paper certificates of marriage or custody are not what make the bond lawful. The promise itself is what matters. Paper may record, but it does not create honour.

In commerce, paperwork is everywhere. Receipts, invoices, contracts, and letters bind parties together. Fraud in any of these is dishonour. To falsify an invoice is theft. To issue false receipts is fraud. To alter contracts secretly is deceit. Sovereigns never engage in such acts. You maintain simple, clear records that reflect truth. If you err, you correct quickly. In this way, paperwork strengthens your honour instead of weakening it.

The maxim commit no fraud is most visible in paperwork and promises. A false word spoken may fade, but a false record endures. It can be used against you years later. That is why honour in paperwork is vital. You never place on record what is not true. You never promise what you cannot do. You never mislead in writing. If forced to sign under duress, you note it. If pressured to agree, you reserve rights. By doing this, you remain sovereign even when systems attempt to bind you.

Across all four nations, paperwork has become the weapon of control. Governments do not seize by sword but by form. Corporations do not enslave by chains but by contracts. Banks do not capture homes with armies but with paperwork. Yet the defence is simple. Live by the maxims. Ask whether the paperwork reflects true harm, true loss, or true fraud. If it does not, it is dishonour. Stand in peace, demand proof, and remain firm.

In conclusion, paperwork and promises are not to be feared but respected. They are tools. Used honourably, they preserve peace. Used dishonourably, they enslave. The sovereign lives by the rule that every word written must be true, every promise made must be kept, and every contract entered must be fair. When this rule is followed, paperwork becomes servant, not master. Promises become strength, not chains. Across America, Canada, the United Kingdom, and Australia, officials may claim power through paper, but truth always outranks ink.

Chapter 9
Money and Credit Illusions

Few subjects cause more confusion and fear than money. Most men and women labour their entire lives chasing paper notes, coins, or digits in an account, believing these things to be wealth. Yet money is not wealth. It is only a symbol of promise. The true wealth is your labour, your time, your creativity, your land, your goods, and your honour. When governments and banks obscure this truth, they create illusions that enslave.

The sovereign must understand these illusions to remain free. Money is perhaps the most common tool of fraud in the modern world. It is used to bind men and women into contracts they never knowingly accepted. It is used to trick them into working for paper created from nothing. It is used to cause loss by draining value through inflation and interest. To see through this, you must hold firmly to the maxims. Do no harm, cause no loss, commit no fraud. When applied to money, they strip away illusion and reveal truth.

In America, the Federal Reserve issues notes that are not backed by gold or silver but by debt. In Canada, the Bank of Canada operates on the same system. In the United Kingdom, the Bank of England issues currency as debt. In Australia, the Reserve Bank follows the same practice. Across all these lands, money is created not by labour but by signature. A loan at a bank is not funded by deposits. It is created when you sign. Your promise generates credit, and the bank records it as money. This is the foundation of modern fraud.

When you borrow, you believe the bank has given you value. In truth, you gave the value by signing. The bank then charges you interest on your own promise. This is loss by deceit. It is fraud disguised as commerce. Courts admit parts of this truth in cases of unfair lending, but the system persists because people do not question it. The sovereign questions. You ask whether full disclosure was given. You ask whether consent was real. You ask whether fraud is present. If fraud is found, the contract is void in honour.

Another illusion is taxation. In America, the Internal Revenue Service demands payment on income. In Canada, the Canada Revenue Agency does the same. In the United Kingdom, HMRC collects tax. In Australia, the ATO issues demands. All rely on paperwork and presumption. They send notices that appear mandatory, but obligation is rarely explained. Few men or women ever ask for proof of harm, loss, or fraud. Instead, they pay out of fear. Yet tax without consent is tribute. Tribute without harm or loss is dishonour. Sovereignty demands that you question every claim.

Inflation is another form of fraud. Governments create more currency, reducing the value of what you hold. Your savings lose power while debts remain. This is loss without consent. No statute can make it honourable. It harms all who labour honestly while benefiting those who create money from nothing. Across America, Canada, the United Kingdom, and Australia, inflation has robbed generations. The sovereign sees it for what it is: hidden theft.

Credit is also illusion. To live on borrowed money is to trade freedom for debt. Credit cards, mortgages, and loans all appear to offer prosperity, yet they bind men and women in chains. A sovereign avoids unnecessary credit. You live within your means, you honour your promises, and you refuse to enter fraudulent agreements. If you must borrow, you demand full disclosure and clear terms. You do not deceive yourself that credit is wealth.

Consider how loss is caused through interest. If you borrow one hundred, you may pay back two hundred. The bank provided nothing of real value, yet you labour double. This is loss inflicted through deceit. In honour, if a man lends value, he may expect value in return. But when nothing is lent and debt is created by trick, charging interest is fraud. Sovereignty means refusing to accept such contracts as lawful.

Another illusion is that governments own the money supply. In truth, private banks control creation. In America, the Federal Reserve is a private system. In Canada, private banks create most credit. In the United Kingdom and Australia, the same is true. The state cooperates, but the mechanism is private. This fraud persists because men and women confuse government authority with bank practice. Sovereigns understand the difference.

Money is also used as a weapon of control. Bank accounts can be frozen, wages garnished, and property seized. These actions are justified by paperwork, not proof of harm. When banks or agencies act without consent, they cause loss. When they conceal their true authority, they commit fraud. The sovereign challenges such acts not with violence but with questions. Where is the contract? Where is the consent? Where is the harm proven? If none can be shown, dishonour lies with the claimant.

Another key point is that money itself carries no moral value. It is not good or evil. It is a tool. The dishonour comes in how it is created and used. To trade honestly with money is fine. To hoard or exploit with it may cause loss. To create it by fraud is dishonour. The sovereign treats money as servant, never as master. You do not measure yourself by paper or digits. You measure yourself by honour.

The illusion of money is strongest because it is reinforced daily. Wages are paid in digits, taxes are demanded in currency, shops exchange only notes or cards. Because every part of life is tied to money, men and women rarely question its nature. Yet when asked directly what money is, most cannot answer. They say it is paper, or coins, or balance in a bank. Few realise that it is only trust, only record of promise. The sovereign understands this, and because of that understanding, fear fades.

Fear of money is what enslaves. People stay in jobs they despise because they fear losing income. They submit to unlawful demands because they fear fines. They obey harmful rules because they fear penalties. All of this fear comes from belief that paper or digits are survival itself. But true survival is in your skills, your community, your land, your ability to live in peace. Money is only a token that represents these. If the tokens are manipulated, your real wealth remains.

Governments and banks exploit this fear. In America, agencies freeze accounts for tax disputes. In Canada, banks report transactions to authorities. In the United Kingdom, benefits are withheld as punishment. In Australia, welfare payments are used to control behaviour. All of these use money as weapon. Yet they can only succeed if you believe that money is your master. The sovereign refuses this illusion. You remember that honour, not digits, sustains you.

Another illusion is national debt. Politicians in every country claim that the nation is in debt to banks. They use this as excuse to raise taxes and cut services. Yet the debt is created by signatures on paper, not by real value lent. In America, trillions are owed to the Federal Reserve. In Canada, billions are owed to lenders. In the United Kingdom and Australia, similar debts exist. But who created them? Men and women did, by signing promises to pay back what never existed. This is fraud on a national scale. Sovereigns see it clearly.

Inflation, as mentioned earlier, is another hidden theft. If you save honestly, you expect value to remain. But each year, the same notes buy less. This is loss caused by deceit. No thief has entered your home, but your wealth is stolen. In America, inflation has destroyed purchasing power of the dollar by over ninety percent in a century. In Canada, the same erosion is clear. In the United Kingdom, the pound has shrunk steadily. In Australia, the dollar's value has fallen. All show that money created from nothing eventually destroys itself.

Credit illusions also trap families. A mortgage is sold as ownership, but until the final payment, the bank holds control. A car loan is sold as freedom, but the lender can seize at will. Credit cards are sold as convenience, but interest traps borrowers for life. Each is presented as opportunity, yet each is bondage. The sovereign recognises that true ownership comes only when no other man or woman holds claim. Until then, paperwork governs, not peace.

Remedy is possible, but it begins with truth. You admit that money is illusion. You admit that banks lend promises, not value. You admit that taxation without consent is tribute. Once admitted, you no longer live in fear. You may still use money for exchange, but you are not ruled by it. You may still pay tax when compelled, but you know it is not lawful claim. You may still borrow if needed, but you do so with open eyes, knowing the fraud beneath. This knowledge restores peace.

Communities throughout history have created their own systems of exchange when central money failed. In America, local currencies have risen during crises. In Canada, barter networks continue. In the United Kingdom, time banks trade hours instead of pounds. In Australia, local exchange trading systems flourish. These show that men and women do not need central banks to trade. Sovereigns participate in such systems to reduce dependence on fraudulent money.

Another important point is generosity. Money loses its power when shared freely. To give without fear is to show mastery over illusion. Hoarding strengthens the fraud. Sharing weakens it. Sovereigns are not careless with resources, but they are generous with surplus. They know that true wealth lies in honour and community, not digits.

Fraud in money is exposed when questions are asked. Ask a banker where the funds came from. Ask a tax officer for proof of obligation. Ask a politician who created the debt. Most cannot answer without exposing fraud. This is why sovereigns use notices and questions. You are not refusing without cause. You are seeking truth. Fraud cannot survive light.

The maxim do no harm applies here too. If you exploit others with money, you harm. If you lend at crushing interest, you cause loss. If you deceive in finance, you commit fraud. Sovereignty requires you to treat money dealings with the same honour as any other matter. You lend fairly. You repay honestly. You trade truthfully. In this way you remove poison from commerce.

Across America, Canada, the United Kingdom, and Australia, courts have admitted that fraud vitiates contracts, that undisclosed commissions void agreements, that misrepresentation destroys obligations. These admissions are cracks in the illusion. Sovereigns widen the cracks by living in honour and refusing to be bound by fraud.

In conclusion, money and credit are the grandest illusions of our age. They enslave not by chains but by paper. Yet the chains break the moment you see them. The sovereign knows that wealth is not digits but labour, not notes but community, not accounts but honour. When you live by the maxims, money loses its power over you. You use it when needed, but you never serve it. You borrow only in truth, trade only in peace, and measure wealth only in freedom. The illusions dissolve, and sovereignty remains.

Chapter 10
Raising Children in Honour

Sovereignty is not a private treasure to be hidden. It is a way of life that must be passed to the next generation. If children are raised to obey without thought, to sign without question, and to trust authority more than conscience, then sovereignty dies within a single lifetime. But if children are raised in honour, taught to live by the maxims, and shown by example how to stand as living men and women, then sovereignty will outlast every statute and every system.

Children learn by imitation more than by lecture. A parent who speaks of freedom but lies in daily dealings teaches fraud. A parent who warns against submission but cheats in trade teaches loss. A parent who tells children to resist authority but shouts angrily at neighbours teaches harm. Children see hypocrisy at once. They may not know the word, but they know dishonour. If you wish to raise sovereign children, you must live sovereignty yourself. Your speech must be truthful. Your promises must be kept. Your dealings must be fair. Children who see this consistency will carry it into their own lives.

In America, Canada, the United Kingdom, and Australia, children are trained from early years to accept authority without question. Schools teach compliance. They teach children to line up, to ask permission for natural needs, to obey bells rather than their own rhythm. They reward silence more than curiosity. They punish questions that challenge. This is not education but conditioning. It prepares children to accept paperwork and promises without reflection. Sovereign parents must resist this conditioning by teaching at home the maxims of honour.

Teaching do no harm begins in the simplest acts. A child who strikes another must be shown the harm caused. A child who speaks cruel words must be guided to see how speech wounds. Punishment alone is not enough. The lesson is not fear of penalty but recognition of harm. When children learn to see others as living men and women with equal dignity, they learn sovereignty.

Teaching cause no loss begins with property. If a child takes what is not theirs, you show the loss caused. If they break what belongs to another, you guide them to repair or replace it. Again, the lesson is not fear of punishment but honour in remedy. When children learn to respect property and to restore what they damage, they learn sovereignty.

Teaching commit no fraud begins with speech. If a child lies, you do not merely punish but show the consequence. Lies destroy trust. Once trust is lost, peace is broken. The remedy is confession and truth. When children learn that honesty restores peace, they learn sovereignty.

These lessons must be lived daily. They cannot be taught once in a lecture. Every incident of harm, loss, or fraud becomes a teaching moment. Sovereign parents do not ignore dishonour, but they also do not rule by fear. They teach by example and explanation. The child learns not only the rules but the reasons. This builds conscience, not mere obedience.

In every jurisdiction, governments claim authority over children. In America, schools impose policies that override parents. In Canada, agencies intervene in family disputes. In the United Kingdom, councils hold powers over education and welfare. In Australia, child protection agencies often overreach. Sovereign parents must know how to navigate these systems. You do not need to be combative. You simply hold your position in honour. You ask questions. You refuse to consent blindly. You protect your children by standing firm in truth.

Children also learn sovereignty through responsibility. Give them tasks appropriate to their age. Let them care for property, share in commerce, and participate in community. A child who grows food, trades fairly, and resolves disputes learns by doing. In America, homesteads once raised children this way. In Canada, rural families taught responsibility early. In the United Kingdom, apprenticeships trained youth in skill and honour. In Australia, farm work did the same. These traditions built sovereignty because they trained children to see themselves as responsible beings, not dependents of the state.

Another important lesson is financial honesty. Children must learn early that money is not magic but promise. Teach them that debt without disclosure is fraud. Teach them that spending without means is loss. Teach them that hoarding while others suffer may cause harm. Give them small sums and let them make choices. Guide them to see the results. Sovereign children grow into sovereign adults when they learn that every coin and contract reflects honour.

Community is also a classroom. Children see how adults treat neighbours. If they see gossip, fraud, and dishonour, they will imitate it. If they see remedy, honesty, and peace, they will imitate that instead. Bring children into community dealings. Let them see disputes resolved by dialogue. Let them see promises kept. Let them witness remedy. By doing so, you train them to expect honour as normal.

In family, promises are vital. Parents must keep their word. If you promise to spend time, you do so. If you promise discipline, you follow through. Broken promises teach fraud. Sovereign families live by promises as sacred bonds. Children who grow in such homes will respect their own word.

Sovereign parents must also guard what influences their children. Schools, media, and peers often reinforce dishonour. Television celebrates fraud disguised as cleverness. Social media encourages envy and deceit. Classrooms reward memorisation of rules rather than discovery of truth. If parents do not provide counterbalance, children will absorb dishonour as normal. You cannot shield them from every influence, but you can equip them to see through illusion. Teach them to ask the same questions you ask: has harm been caused, has loss been inflicted, has fraud been committed? This simple framework allows them to cut through deception wherever they encounter it.

Another challenge is authority outside the home. Teachers, police, or officials may give instructions that conflict with conscience. A child trained only to obey will submit. A sovereign child will pause, ask questions, and stand in truth. This does not mean rudeness. Honour requires respect in speech. But it does mean courage. Teach your children that they are living men and women, not property of the state. Teach them that officials are also men and women bound by the maxims. By doing so, you prepare them for encounters where honour will be tested.

Consider how differently societies would look if every child were raised with sovereignty. Bullying in schools would vanish because children would see harm clearly and refuse to cause it. Theft among peers would dissolve because they would know it as loss and seek remedy. Lies would diminish because children would understand fraud as dishonour. Communities would grow in peace because each generation would carry the maxims naturally. The reason governments expand control is because men and women forget these truths. To restore them, start with children.

Discipline is another area where sovereignty matters. Many parents confuse discipline with punishment. Punishment is fear-based control. Discipline is guidance into honour. When a child errs, punishment alone teaches only to avoid being caught. Discipline teaches the why. You explain the harm, show the loss, reveal the fraud. Then you guide the child to remedy. This builds conscience rather than fear. Sovereign discipline is firm but never cruel, corrective but never degrading.

Examples help children learn. When you make mistakes, admit them openly. If you speak harshly, confess and apologise. If you break a promise, acknowledge and restore. By doing this, you show that sovereignty is not perfection but honesty. Children who see parents admit fault learn to do the same. They learn that honour is preserved not by never failing but by always making remedy.

Sovereign parenting also prepares children for financial independence. Teach them early to work, trade, and save. Show them that labour is property, not to be given away without honour. Teach them that debt is bondage when fraudulent. Encourage them to avoid credit illusions. Give them chances to earn and spend responsibly. Across America, Canada, the United Kingdom, and Australia, young people fall into debt traps because no one taught them truth. Sovereign families break this cycle by raising children who see through financial fraud.

Family traditions can reinforce sovereignty. Set aside times to review the maxims together. Share stories of honour from history and community. Celebrate acts of truth and remedy. Create rituals of honesty, such as weekly family meetings where everyone speaks openly. These practices teach children that sovereignty is not only theory but lived daily.

Raising children in honour also means preparing them to face hardship. Life will test them with temptation, pressure, and fear. If they know only comfort, they may break under trial. But if they are trained in patience, service, and courage, they will endure. In America, pioneer children learned sovereignty through labour. In Canada, northern families taught survival skills. In the United Kingdom, apprentices learned responsibility through craft. In Australia, outback families taught children to endure isolation. All these built strength. Modern parents must find ways to teach resilience, even in cities. Sovereignty thrives in strong character.

One of the greatest gifts parents can give is literacy in record. Teach children to read contracts, notices, and forms with care. Teach them to ask for meaning of words. Teach them never to sign without understanding. If they learn this young, they will not be trapped as adults. Many men and women fall into dishonour because they signed blindly. Sovereign children will not. They will know that every signature is a promise and every promise must be honoured.

Another gift is skill in speech. Children must learn to speak truth calmly, even under pressure. Role-play encounters with teachers, employers, or officials. Teach them to ask questions respectfully. Teach them to refuse dishonour without anger. These habits will protect them when they face real challenges. In every jurisdiction, those who speak clearly and calmly are respected, even by officials. Sovereign children carry this strength with them.

In closing, raising children in honour is the most important duty of sovereignty. Without the next generation, sovereignty ends. But with children trained in the maxims, sovereignty grows stronger each decade. They will live in honour, pass it to their children, and slowly restore peace to communities. You cannot change nations overnight, but you can change your family today. By teaching do no harm, cause no loss, commit no fraud, you give children a compass that no government can erase.

Chapter 11

Building Private Agreements

Sovereignty does not mean isolation. Men and women live in relationship. They trade, share, borrow, lend, and cooperate. Every one of these acts is an agreement. Some agreements are formal and written, others are spoken, some are sealed only by a handshake. Whether large or small, whether involving money or simply trust, agreements bind people together. The question is whether they are honourable.

Governments insist that all important agreements must pass through their systems. They require licences, registrations, and taxes. They claim that without their approval, agreements are invalid. But this is not true. Long before parliaments and statutes, men and women made agreements privately and honoured them. Villages were built, markets thrived, and families prospered on private agreements alone. Sovereignty means remembering that this is still possible.

An agreement is honourable when it meets the maxims. No harm is caused. No loss is inflicted. No fraud is committed. If these conditions are satisfied, the agreement is lawful in truth, whether or not it is recognised by the state. In America, contracts formed privately are still enforceable if meeting minds can be shown. In Canada, oral agreements carry legal force if witnesses exist. In the United Kingdom, handshake deals have stood in courts for centuries. In Australia, private contracts are valid under common law. Across all jurisdictions, the principle remains: agreement is born of consent, not of state permission.

Private agreements thrive on clarity. Fraud enters when terms are hidden or vague. Loss arises when one side expects more than the other offered. Harm follows when resentment grows. A sovereign avoids this by speaking plainly. If you lend money, state the amount and the terms. If you share property, state how it may be used. If you exchange labour, state what will be provided. Write it down in simple words if necessary. Complexity is not strength. Clarity is.

Witness is another safeguard. In every culture, agreements were once witnessed by neighbours or elders. This simple act discouraged fraud and preserved peace. In America, notaries public serve this role. In Canada, commissioners of oaths perform similar duties. In the United Kingdom and Australia, affidavits and witnessed signatures provide strength. But you do not need officials. A trusted friend or family member can serve as witness. The point is record, not bureaucracy.

Private agreements also extend to community projects. Families may pool resources to buy land. Neighbours may form co-operatives to share equipment. Friends may create private associations for mutual aid. In all these cases, honour is the key. If promises are kept, peace thrives. If fraud or loss enters, conflict follows. Sovereigns know that private agreements work best when rooted in the maxims.

Consider a lending circle. A group of friends each contribute money, and in turn each borrows in rotation. Such circles exist in America, Canada, the United Kingdom, and Australia under many names. They succeed not because of government oversight but because members honour promises. Fraud destroys them. Loss without remedy breaks them. But when honour rules, such agreements provide freedom from banks and officials.

Another form is barter. Two men exchange goods or services without money. One repairs a roof, the other provides food. If both keep promises, the agreement is lawful and peaceful. If one cheats, dishonour arises. No statute is needed to enforce remedy. The community sees dishonour and withdraws trust. In this way, private agreements regulate themselves through reputation. Sovereigns rely on this natural enforcement rather than state power.

Private agreements also govern family. Marriage, inheritance, and care for children are all agreements in truth. Governments intrude with licences and courts, but families may manage these privately. A man and woman can promise fidelity without paper. Parents can promise provision to children without forms. Brothers and sisters can agree on inheritance without probate. The key is honour. If promises are kept, peace remains. Fraud and loss invite interference.

Across history, private agreements have built nations. In America, pioneers relied on contracts of trust to survive. In Canada, fur traders made deals without state oversight. In the United Kingdom, guilds organised work through private rules. In Australia, settlers built communities by mutual promise. All these thrived without state regulation. They show that sovereignty in agreements is not theory but tradition.

The sovereign today must revive this practice. Do not assume that every agreement must pass through government. Build agreements privately where possible. Keep them clear, truthful, and fair. Use witnesses. Keep simple records. Honour promises. In doing so, you reduce dependence on officials and strengthen community.

Private agreements also protect sovereignty in commerce. When you buy from a neighbour directly, you avoid middlemen, banks, and state interference. A clear receipt or handshake is enough. If you sell your produce or labour in peace, no official is required to validate the exchange. This is why farmers' markets, co-operatives, and barter networks flourish in America, Canada, the United Kingdom, and Australia. They thrive not because of statute but because of trust. Each trade is a private agreement based on honour.

Fraud in private agreements is especially damaging because it poisons trust. When one member of a community cheats, all become cautious. This is why remedy is vital. If you fail in a promise, admit it quickly and restore what is owed. Sovereigns do not hide mistakes. They correct them. This builds a reputation stronger than any licence. Men and women will choose to deal with you again because they know your word is reliable.

Private agreements can also shield you from exploitation. For example, a group of families may form a private trust to educate their children. They agree on contributions, curriculum, and duties. By doing this, they reduce dependence on government schools and preserve sovereignty. In America, homeschooling co-operatives are based on such agreements. In Canada, private associations provide similar alternatives. In the United Kingdom, home education groups rely on parental contracts. In Australia, families form learning communities. These agreements show that men and women can govern themselves without state intrusion.

Insurance is another area where private agreements once prevailed. Neighbours pooled resources to help if disaster struck. In America, mutual aid societies flourished. In Canada, friendly societies provided support. In the United Kingdom, community funds offered security. In Australia, bush communities created informal safety nets. All were private agreements based on honour. Today, corporations dominate insurance with complex contracts and hidden terms. Yet private arrangements can still exist when men and women trust each other and live by the maxims.

Marriage is perhaps the most personal private agreement. Governments claim authority over it through licences, yet the union itself is a promise between man and woman. Sovereigns understand that the paper does not create the bond. The bond is created by promise and honour. Likewise, inheritance is a private agreement. Families can decide distribution in peace. Courts intrude only when dishonour arises. If promises are kept and records are clear, sovereignty is preserved.

Private agreements are also a form of defence against state overreach. Governments regulate commerce, family, and property through licences and permits. By creating private agreements, men and women bypass this intrusion. For example, a private association can allow trade among members without state interference. As long as all parties consent and honour promises, the agreement is lawful in truth. In America, private membership associations are used for health, food, and education. In Canada, private societies serve the same purpose. In the United Kingdom and Australia, similar models are growing. These examples show how sovereignty thrives when people agree privately to live by honour.

Another strength of private agreements is flexibility. Statutes are rigid and slow to change. Private agreements can be tailored to circumstance. If neighbours want to share water rights, they can craft terms specific to their land. If families want to pool resources for housing, they can set rules that suit them. Flexibility is only limited by imagination and honour. Fraud and dishonour ruin agreements. Truth and fairness sustain them.

The principle of witness deserves emphasis. When agreements are witnessed, fraud becomes harder. In America, affidavits and notarisation serve this role. In Canada, sworn declarations provide the same. In the United Kingdom and Australia, signatures with witnesses create strength. Sovereigns use witnesses not because statutes demand it but because it protects honour. Two men may agree privately, but a third who observes adds weight. This simple habit prevents dispute.

Record also strengthens private agreements. Keep copies of promises, payments, and terms. A notebook, a ledger, or a signed paper is enough. In every jurisdiction, record is treated as proof. But even if courts are not involved, record preserves peace. It shows what was agreed and prevents memory from causing fraud. Sovereigns understand that clear record is not bureaucracy but honour.

Trust is the foundation of private agreements. Without trust, no agreement lasts. Trust is earned through consistency. If you keep your word, others will deal with you again. If you break it, they withdraw. Sovereigns guard their reputation fiercely. Your word is your wealth. One broken promise can cause more loss than coins ever could. Across all nations, men and women remember who is honourable. Your name becomes either trusted or avoided. Sovereignty means ensuring it is trusted.

Finally, private agreements remind us that law is not complicated. You do not need libraries of statute to live in peace. Two or more men and women can agree to terms, keep them, and restore if they fail. That is the whole of it. Governments add layers of regulation to gain power and profit. Sovereigns strip it back to the maxims. Honour your agreements. Do no harm. Cause no loss. Commit no fraud. If you live this way, your community thrives without endless interference.

In conclusion, building private agreements is one of the strongest acts of sovereignty. It proves that men and women can live by honour without the state. It demonstrates that trust is more powerful than licences. It shows that peace comes from promises kept, not from threats of penalty. Across America, Canada, the United Kingdom, and Australia, private agreements continue quietly, sustaining families and communities. They are the hidden foundation of freedom. By reviving and multiplying them, sovereign men and women secure a future where honour governs daily life.

Chapter 12

The Daily Practice of Sovereignty

Sovereignty is not an idea to be discussed only in debate halls or written about in books. It is a way of life. A man or woman does not become sovereign by declaration alone but by daily practice. Every word spoken, every agreement made, every action taken must align with the maxims. Do no harm, cause no loss, commit no fraud. To live them consistently is to live free.

The challenge is that life is full of tests. From morning to night, you are presented with choices. Some are small: how you speak to a neighbour, whether you keep a promise, whether you return what you borrowed. Others are larger: how you handle officials, how you trade in commerce, how you raise your children. Each choice reveals whether you are sovereign or not. Sovereignty is not proven once. It is proven every day.

In the United States, Canada, the United Kingdom, and Australia alike, men and women often feel crushed by the weight of systems. They see governments expanding, corporations dominating, and courts intruding. They believe freedom is lost. Yet sovereignty is not lost unless you abandon it. Even in the most controlled societies, a man or woman who holds to honour is free within. The chains of paperwork cannot bind the conscience. The illusions of money cannot trap the honest heart. The tricks of officials cannot deceive the man who lives in truth.

Daily practice begins with speech. The words you use shape your path. Speak truth and you remain free. Speak lies and you bind yourself. A sovereign trains speech carefully. You do not speak promises you cannot keep. You do not repeat rumours. You do not answer questions that invite dishonour. You speak little but with weight. This habit builds respect in community and strength in self.

The next practice is remedy. No man or woman is perfect. You will harm, you will cause loss, you will fail in promises. Sovereignty is not about never failing but about correcting quickly. If you break something, replace it. If you miss a promise, admit it and restore. If you wound with words, apologise sincerely. This practice keeps you in honour even when you fall. Others see that you take responsibility, and trust grows.

Record is another daily practice. Keep simple notes of agreements, payments, and exchanges. Not to build bureaucracy, but to preserve peace. When disputes arise, record ends confusion. In every jurisdiction, record carries weight. But more importantly, it shows your honour to yourself and to others. A notebook, a ledger, or even memory written down soon after is enough. Sovereigns do not drown in paperwork but keep enough record to prevent fraud.

Questions are another discipline. Officials, neighbours, and traders will make claims. Instead of rushing to agree or argue, you ask questions. Who makes the claim? What harm, loss, or fraud is alleged? What evidence is offered? Who accepts liability if the claim is false? By asking calmly, you shift burden where it belongs. This habit prevents you from stepping into dishonour.

Another practice is patience. The systems of control thrive on haste. They want quick signatures, instant compliance, immediate answers. The sovereign resists this pressure. You take time to read, reflect, and decide. If pressed, you state calmly that you require time. This practice frustrates fraud and preserves peace. Across America, Canada, the United Kingdom, and Australia, officials rely on fear and urgency. Patience removes their power.

Community service is also part of daily practice. Sovereignty is not selfish isolation. It is honour in relationship. Help a neighbour, contribute to projects, share resources fairly. By doing this, you strengthen bonds of trust. When disputes arise, the community remembers your honour and supports you. Sovereignty lived in isolation is fragile. Sovereignty lived in community is strong.

Finally, daily practice requires reflection. Each evening, ask yourself: did I harm, did I cause loss, did I commit fraud? If the answer is yes, plan remedy. If the answer is no, give thanks. This habit trains conscience and sharpens honour. Over time, you become steady. Fear fades, courage grows, peace deepens. This is sovereignty in practice, not theory.

The discipline of sovereignty is simple to describe but difficult to live because dishonour is common in modern life. Entire industries are built on fraud. Advertising exaggerates, banking conceals, politics deceives, and media distorts. To walk in honour requires vigilance. Each day you are tempted to take shortcuts, to mislead for advantage, to ignore harm when it benefits you. The sovereign must refuse these temptations. You do not excuse yourself by pointing to corruption in others. You remain clean regardless of what others do.

Work provides many such tests. Employers may ask you to shade the truth in reports, to sell goods with false claims, or to overlook safety risks. Colleagues may encourage you to cut corners. In these moments, the easy path is dishonour. It promises profit or comfort. The sovereign path is harder. You speak truth, you refuse fraud, you seek remedy for harm. This may cost you promotion or approval, but it preserves your sovereignty. A man or woman who sells honour for wages loses freedom.

Family is another arena of daily practice. It is easy to speak sharply to a spouse, to ignore promises to children, or to conceal errors. Dishonour here may seem small, but it poisons trust at the foundation. Sovereigns treat family with the same care as courts. You keep your word at home. You apologise when wrong. You restore peace quickly. Children and partners who see this consistency learn to trust your word. Without honour in family, sovereignty in public is hollow.

Community interactions test honour constantly. When borrowing tools, when sharing space, when discussing disputes, you must hold the maxims. Do not harm with gossip. Do not cause loss by negligence. Do not commit fraud by misrepresentation. Each small act builds reputation. In America, Canada, the United Kingdom, and Australia alike, reputation has always been more powerful than law. A trusted name opens doors, while a dishonourable one closes them. The sovereign guards reputation as treasure.

Officials also test sovereignty daily. You may receive letters demanding payment, notices threatening penalty, or forms asking for information. Most people comply out of habit or fear. The sovereign responds with calm questions. You never ignore without record, and you never sign without understanding. You place your truth on record and ask claimants to prove theirs. Often they cannot. But even if they proceed, you remain in honour. You have not lied, you have not consented blindly, and you have not submitted in fear.

Another daily practice is restraint. The world provokes anger. Officials insult, neighbours offend, systems frustrate. Anger leads to harsh words, which cause harm. Violence causes greater harm. Sovereignty demands calm. You may feel anger, but you master it. You respond with peace. This is not weakness but strength. In every jurisdiction, those who remain calm under pressure are respected more than those who lash out. The sovereign is known by composure.

Patience is equally vital. Fraud often collapses when exposed to time. Officials send notices but fail to answer questions. Corporations make claims but cannot provide evidence. Courts delay but eventually reveal weakness. The sovereign does not panic. You wait, record, and persist. Time becomes ally. This patience is daily discipline. Without it, fear drives you to dishonour.

Generosity is another daily mark of sovereignty. To give freely of time, skill, or goods without expectation strengthens peace. It proves you are not ruled by money or greed. It shows that honour, not profit, governs you. Communities in every land remember generous men and women long after they forget the wealthy. Generosity also builds networks of trust that protect sovereignty. When trouble comes, those you have helped will stand with you.

Reflection closes the day. You look back honestly. Did you harm, cause loss, or commit fraud? If so, you plan remedy. If not, you give thanks and rest in peace. This practice strengthens conscience. Each day becomes a lesson. Over time, dishonour decreases and honour increases. Sovereignty is not gained overnight. It is built step by step, day by day.

The daily practice also prepares you for greater trials. If you live in honour in small things, you will stand strong in large ones. If you cannot keep a simple promise to a friend, you will not stand before a judge. If you cannot admit a small lie, you will not resist state fraud. Discipline in little matters builds strength for great ones. Sovereigns understand that every act is training.

Across America, Canada, the United Kingdom, and Australia, men and women are awakening to these truths. They see that sovereignty is not rebellion but responsibility. It is not shouting at officials but living cleanly in daily life. It is not refusing every demand but demanding truth in every claim. As more live this way, communities grow in peace. Officials lose power when dishonour is exposed. Fraud weakens when men and women refuse to join it.

The daily practice of sovereignty therefore is the true revolution. Not marches, not riots, not declarations, but steady honour in every act. When enough men and women live this way, systems of fraud collapse naturally. They cannot stand when truth is normal. They cannot deceive when questions are asked. They cannot enslave when promises are honoured privately. Sovereignty spreads by example, not by force.

In closing, remember that sovereignty is not a distant goal but a daily walk. Each morning you choose honour. Each evening you examine yourself. Each word, each promise, each action either strengthens or weakens your freedom. The maxims are not complicated. Do no harm. Cause no loss. Commit no fraud. Live them in every moment and sovereignty becomes not an idea but your very life.

Conclusion

The Three Maxims Are Enough

Sovereignty is not a dream, not a fantasy, not an escape from reality. It is reality itself when lived in honour. The maxims are so simple that many overlook them. They search for secret laws, hidden codes, and complex loopholes. They believe freedom will be found in some forgotten statute or obscure treaty. Yet the truth is before them in plain sight. Do no harm. Cause no loss. Commit no fraud. These three maxims are enough to live free in any land.

Every chapter of this book has shown how these maxims apply. In speech, in property, in commerce, in community, in record, in promises, in money, in raising children, and in daily life, the same rules stand. They cut through confusion. They strip away fear. They expose fraud. They prevent dishonour. They restore peace.

In America, the Constitution and Bill of Rights are often treated as the highest authority. In Canada, the Charter of Rights and Freedoms holds that place. In the United Kingdom, Parliament is claimed to be supreme. In Australia, the Commonwealth Constitution is invoked. Yet none of these texts are higher than conscience. Each in its own way admits this truth by recognising principles of fairness, natural justice, and equity. These principles are only reflections of the maxims. No document, however revered, outranks truth.

History shows that dishonour leads always to collapse. Empires have fallen because rulers harmed their people, stole their property, and deceived with fraud. Rome taxed until rebellion. Monarchies lost trust through lies. Banks collapsed under fraud. Nations went to war to cover dishonour. But communities that lived in peace, respected property, and kept promises endured. Honour sustains. Dishonour destroys. This pattern is visible in every age, in every jurisdiction.

The sovereign does not wait for governments to reform. You live the maxims now. If officials are honourable, you respect them. If they are not, you expose them by questions. If courts are just, you cooperate. If they are not, you stand firm in peace. You do not depend on external reform to live free. Freedom begins in yourself.

The maxims also unite across cultures. Every religion, every tradition, every people recognises them. In Christianity, love your neighbour as yourself reflects them. In Judaism, do not bear false witness, do not steal, do not kill echo them. In Islam, honesty in trade and justice in conduct affirm them. In Buddhism, right speech and right action uphold them. Indigenous traditions across the world teach respect for life, property, and truth. These are not foreign laws but universal conscience.

Living the maxims is not easy. The world tempts with shortcuts. Fraud offers quick gain. Harm promises revenge. Loss tempts with greed. But every time you choose dishonour, you weaken yourself. Every time you choose honour, you strengthen sovereignty. It is a daily battle within, not outside. The enemy is not officials, judges, or corporations. The enemy is the temptation to lie, to cheat, to harm. Master that and you are sovereign no matter what the outside world does.

Sovereignty must also be shared. If you keep it to yourself, its power is limited. When you live in honour openly, others notice. They see your calmness when officials threaten. They see your fairness in trade. They see your consistency in promises. They see your peace when others panic. This example speaks louder than lectures. You do not need to convert by argument. You inspire by conduct. In every community, one sovereign man or woman can influence dozens. In every family, one honourable parent can shape generations.

The maxims also protect against despair. Many men and women who awaken to fraud in government feel overwhelmed. They see corruption everywhere. They fear collapse. They wonder whether resistance is hopeless. But the maxims remind you that freedom does not depend on systems. Even in the darkest times, you can live without harm, without loss, without fraud. No statute, no official, no policy can prevent you from honour. As long as you hold it, you are free inside. And freedom inside always finds ways to manifest outside.

This book has drawn examples from America, Canada, the United Kingdom, and Australia because these lands share traditions of common law and equity. Yet the maxims go beyond legal systems. They apply in every country, every culture, every age. If harm, loss, or fraud is present, dishonour exists. If they are absent, peace exists. It is that simple. Courts may try to complicate. Governments may try to obscure. But truth is not hidden. It is lived.

Practical sovereignty therefore is not a theory to be admired but a practice to be lived. Begin small. Keep every promise today. Speak only truth today. Refuse to harm today. Replace what you damage today. Correct what you misstate today. One day becomes two. Two become ten. Ten become habit. Habits become life. Sovereignty is built not by speeches but by consistent honour.

Sovereigns also recognise that remedy is more powerful than punishment. Governments punish. They fine, imprison, or shame. But punishment often breeds more dishonour. Remedy restores peace. When harm occurs, repair it. When loss occurs, restore it. When fraud occurs, confess and correct it. This approach heals rather than divides. It keeps communities strong and families united. It creates peace that no official can impose.

The maxims are also weapons of defence. When officials threaten, you ask calmly: what harm, what loss, what fraud? If they cannot answer, they have no lawful claim. When corporations deceive, you demand proof. If none is given, their fraud is exposed. When neighbours quarrel, you call them back to the maxims. These questions are shields. They cut through illusion and restore clarity.

To conclude, sovereignty is not gained by secret codes, not preserved by endless documents, not granted by rulers. It is lived by honour. If you live by the three maxims, you are sovereign already. If you do not, no declaration will make you free. Do no harm. Cause no loss. Commit no fraud. These are enough. They have always been enough. They will always be enough.

The challenge now belongs to you. Read these words, but more importantly, live them. Apply them in family, in work, in community, in dealings with officials, in record, in promises, in money. Teach them to your children. Model them in your conduct. Share them by example. In this way, sovereignty spreads quietly but powerfully. Fraud collapses. Fear fades. Peace grows.

The world will not change overnight. But each act of honour is a seed. Plant enough seeds and a forest rises. Live the maxims daily, and sovereignty becomes not theory but reality. And when enough men and women live this way, no government, no bank, no court can stand against it. Honour will prevail.

Don't miss out!

Visit the website below and you can sign up to receive emails whenever Roger Davies publishes a new book. There's no charge and no obligation.

https://books2read.com/r/B-A-HHGNE-WHRYG

BOOKS 2 READ

Connecting independent readers to independent writers.

Did you love *The Definitive Sovereign Handbook: Do No Harm, Cause No Loss, Commit No Fraud*? Then you should read *Sovereign Stories for Children: 14 Parables of Freedom, Truth, and Honour*[1] by Roger Davies!

[2]

What do you want your children to carry into their future, fear of authority, or confidence in truth? Blind obedience, or the strength to ask questions?

Sovereign Stories for Children: 14 Parables of Freedom, Truth, and Honour is written for parents like you who want to raise children with courage, wisdom, and a clear sense of right and wrong. This book is not another fairy tale about kings and castles where power always wins. It is a collection of parables designed to teach the core values of the Sovereign way of life in a way that even a child under ten can grasp.

Every story is short enough to read aloud at bedtime, but deep enough to spark conversations that matter. In these 14 tales, your child will meet:

1. https://books2read.com/u/bpPxB9

2. https://books2read.com/u/bpPxB9

• A nightingale who refuses to carry papers to sing in the open sky.• A farmer who delivers an empty basket when unjust tax collectors come.• A lion who remembers he was always free, no matter what cage he once knew.• A child who questions the Crown and speaks truth stronger than banners.• Neighbours who reclaim a bridge from toll keepers by asking for proof.• And many more fables that show the difference between rules made by power and law written in honour.

Each chapter ends with questions for you to ask together and a short moral in simple words. This makes it easy for your child to reflect on what they've heard and for you to guide them in seeing how the lesson applies to real life.

Why is this book different? Because it is not about fantasy kingdoms or talking animals for amusement alone. It is about planting seeds of Sovereign thinking early — teaching your child that true law is not whatever someone writes on paper, but the timeless principles every honest man, woman, and child already knows:

Do no harm.Cause no loss.Do not lie.Ask for proof.

By sharing these stories, you give your child tools to stand strong in a world that often demands silence and obedience. You give them confidence to question claims that have no proof. You remind them that they already carry the law of truth inside themselves.

The benefits are not only for your child. These stories also remind you, as a parent, of the strength you carry when you live free from fear and in honour with your neighbours. Reading aloud together builds bonds of trust and gives you language to speak about freedom in ways that are simple but lasting.

Imagine your child remembering these lessons when faced with peer pressure, false authority, or unfair demands. Instead of bowing, they will know to ask: *"Where is the promise that binds me?"* That question alone is powerful enough to change the path of their whole life.

This book belongs on the shelf of every family who values freedom. It is a guide you can return to again and again, not only as a set of bedtime stories but as a foundation for raising the next generation of Sovereign men and women.

If you want your children to grow up brave, honourable, and awake to truth, this is the book to start with.

Read it with them. Talk about it with them. Live it with them.

Freedom is not given. It is remembered. And it begins in the heart of a child.

Also by Roger Davies

Adventures in Sovereignty: Growing Up Free
The Secret of the Hidden Name

Sovereign Foundations: Liberty, Rights, Consent
The Constitution of One: How the Bill of Rights Protects the Sovereign Man & Woman
From Subjects to Sovereigns: Reclaiming the Spirit of 1776
Liberty by Consent: Reclaiming Freedom Through the Law of Consent

Standalone
The Commonwealth Corporation: How Australia Was Turned Into a Business
The Legal Fiction: The Greatest Trick Ever Played on Humanity
The Sovereign Path: Living Free Beyond the System
Common Law: The True Law of the Living
Freedom by Rebuttal: How to Say No and Stand Free
The Magna Carta: Why It Is Important to Sovereign Men and Women
The Trust Game: Hidden Estates and the Cestui Que Vie Act
Freedom by Notice: Winning with Paperwork
The Hidden Contracts: How Governments Enslave the People
The Law of the Living: Admiralty Shadows and the Path to Sovereignty
Standing as a Living Man or Woman in Canada: Reclaiming Freedom Beyond Statutes and Policy

Sovereign Stories for Children: 14 Parables of Freedom, Truth, and Honour

The Definitive Sovereign Handbook: Do No Harm, Cause No Loss, Commit No Fraud

About the Author

Roger Davies researches the crossroads of commerce, policy, and personal sovereignty. He writes for readers who sense there is more to the story, who are ready to replace fear with honour and paperwork with plain truth. When not writing, he helps men and women organise their records, challenge unfounded claims, and build communities grounded in mutual aid and responsibility.